PRACTICAL PIGEON SHOOTING

PRACTICAL PIGEON SHOOTING

PETER HALL

The Crowood Press

First published in 1995 by
The Crowood Press Ltd
Ramsbury, Marlborough
Wiltshire SN8 2HR

British Library Cataloguing-in-Publication Data
A catalogue record for this book is available from the British Library.

ISBN 1 85223 864 X

Line drawings by Paul Groombridge
Photographs by the author and Will Garfit

Photograph on page 2: The author

Designed and typeset by
D & N Publishing
DTP & Editorial Services
The Stable Block
Crowood Lane
Ramsbury
Wiltshire SN8 2HR

Printed and bound by The Bath Press
Typeface: M Plantin

CONTENTS

1 SPORT FOR ALL

I was a very young boy when the keeper on my local Estate gave me an old hammer-gun and fifty or so cartridges and told me to get up to the wood to have a pot at the woodpigeons that would be coming in with the dusk. I can remember it all now, years on, as clear as day, it was a biting cold evening, and I trudged over the hard ground and took up my place as he told me. The wind howling at my back, I was hidden by the fringe of the wood. I was in a hollow in the ground, and there was a great old fallen tree in front of me – an ideal place, though I hardly knew it then.

As the light went, so the snow came in – a great old blizzard raging and freezing me so that my teeth chattered. There were no warm clothes in those days, and it would not surprise me if I even had short trousers on despite the freezing temperatures. The pigeons seemed to love it, coming in quickly

Portrait of a country sportsman!

The old keepers' shed – they knew everything about pigeons there ever was to know.

through the snow flakes, so close that even I could not miss. Bang, bang, bang! Down they went until it was just too dark to carry on any longer.

I got out of my hiding place and wandered around looking for the fallen birds. I thought that I had been successful with virtually every shot, and I was wild with excitement. In the end I picked up six perhaps but no more. I was near tears. I just couldn't understand it and had to troop back to the keeper with only a handful of pigeons, fearing the worst.

I needn't have worried: the old keeper just laughed and told me that there would be plenty out there, lying dead but hidden under the snow. He was right too. By the next morning when the snow had thawed a little, I could see lots of wings exposed, and I was happy again!

Of course, you couldn't and wouldn't send a boy out alone with a gun now, certainly not on a night like that. None the less, I survived, and I learned a lot – not least to love pigeon shooting more than anything else in the sporting world. As a lad, that was all the shooting I could get, and I was given a lot of encouragement. Old George Lamb (long since dead) was the keeper, and he taught me everything before he passed away. He'd say, 'Come and see me if there's anything at all you want to know, lad,' and that's how I learned from him.

In many ways everything is just the same today. There cannot be a better bird than the pigeon for any youngster or novice to begin shooting. Pheasant or partridge shoots, stalking, or even wildfowling are very expensive. Including travel expenses, these types of shooting can cost more than an average weekly wage per day, perhaps a lot more. Pigeons, on the other hand, are a pest – a real problem for farmers who see their crops half destroyed by flocks of the birds. A polite request for shooting will, therefore, only very rarely be refused. In the old days, some farmers would even give you the cartridges!

There is no better shooting bird than the pigeon. It flies both quickly and unpredictably, and it has superb eyesight. Old George used to say that a pigeon could see as well as a hawk, and I have come to believe him. If you learn to shoot pigeons, no other bird will give you any trouble later on. You are really up against a wild and a wary bird when you face the pigeon.

I have heard it said that young guns are well started off with clay pigeons. That may be true, but clays are not cheap, and – even more important in my view – they always fly predictably. You don't see them dip and swoop and change direction in mid-flight like the real birds. Of course clay pigeon shooting has many great things going for it, but in my view it cannot come close to the thrill of being out in a wood in the late afternoon or the excitement of preparing a hide.

I always like to think that the pigeon is the real countryman's bird. Once you get to know country people, you will find them a great help when it comes to a bit of pigeon shooting. Foresters, keepers, farm workers and even postmen will all keep their eyes open and will be happy to tell you

In inclement weather, the pigeons will have to work hard for their food.

Any bird – pigeon or partridge – will look for a good vantage point.

Let's say you're roost shooting. You might well see the deer beginning to move out of the wood to feed as you walk home with a few birds in your bag. If you're not a real naturalist to start with then you'll soon become one if you are a pigeon shot. For that reason alone, I can't think of a better excuse to take youngsters out for a bit of sport.

Furthermore, after a great day, when you come back tired but happy, you will have something to eat as well. You can even sell any surplus to cover costs, but I like to think you'll give them away too. Any pigeon that you don't need would probably be much appreciated by others. That's why I call pigeon shooting 'sport for all': you have your sport, the farmer is rid of some pests and friends get their Sunday lunch. Nothing's wasted, and that's how it should be in the country. The pigeon is a lovely bird, and it will not be long before you begin to appreciate him in all his moods, in all weathers and in all types of countryside.

Pigeons come in all shapes and sizes!

where pigeons are working and on what crops they are feeding at that particular time. Once you become known in the area, you'll even find the farmer will ring up to ask if you will come over and help him out.

Any real pigeon shot loves to get down in his hide, his eyes skinned, just waiting. It's amazing the things one sees over a lifetime. Best of all you'll see a fox going home or a badger snuffling along the hedgerow, stopping here and there, scratching up voles or beetles for its cubs back in the set. If you are well hidden and the wind is right, you might even have them scratching on your hide!

2 THE WAY THINGS WERE

The old days on a farm when one man would hold vermin culling duties.

I suppose in some ways I should have entitled this chapter 'The Bad Old Days' or something like that because it doesn't show man in a very positive light. In fact, I only include this chapter to show how things have improved when it comes to humanitarian behaviour. The incident that I am going to describe, I think, also shows how clay pigeon shooting began.

I was a very young lad at the time, and I still recall the occasion with some excitement. I can't remember all the details now, because time has made them very hazy indeed, but at least it's still there in my memory. I was taken to a piece of farmland one late spring evening, where there was a whole crowd of people, some of whom I knew vaguely or at least had seen in my area. As I remember, there were five mechanical traps positioned to form a large circle. The traps were about five or six yards apart, and I remember realizing that there was a pigeon sitting in each one.

Early metal powder flasks.

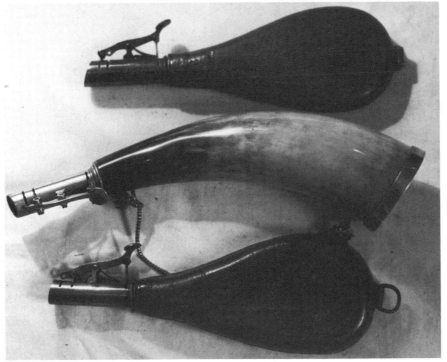

Early powder flasks of leather and horn.

There was a great deal of drinking and talking and general excitement, and several people were walking around with guns. I suspect that betting was also taking place. All in all, it was the sort of wild scene that you'd expect to find amongst working countrymen virtually half a century ago.

Several men took it in turns to shoot the pigeons, which were released quite haphazardly as far as I can remember by a man pulling a piece of string outside the circle. Any one of the five cages would open, and a pigeon would immediately fly out and try to gain height before the poor thing was shot.

There were plenty of rows as I recall – not so much as to whether each pigeon was getting killed because that was pretty self-evident, but about where the thing fell or where it had been shot in the air. That side of things seemed to be very important indeed, and to score maximum points the gun had to shoot the bird within a pre-scribed time or distance.

As I was barely a child, I found the whole thing very exciting, but now obviously I'd look on it with horror. I'm not at all sure when this type of 'sport' was outlawed, but I guess it must have been a fair time ago. In fact, it could well have been illegal then, in the 1930s, for the meeting took place well away from any habitation.

Today, there's a great deal of enthusiasm for clay pigeon shooting, and whenever I talk to anybody about that branch of the sport, I think back all those years to its probable origins, with a bit of a thrill as well as a certain amount of disgust.

Right towards the end of the meeting, I was actually allowed to take part and pull the string that released one of the pigeons to its certain death. At the time, I considered it a very great honour indeed, and I went home flushed with pride – and with a couple of coppers clinking away in my pocket. I suppose it was an accumulation of small things like that which made me as keen on field sports as I am today.

Many years ago, the blunderbuss was used to scare pigeons off the fields.

3 A PROFILE OF THE PIGEON

Columba palumbus, the ring dove, the wood-pigeon, the woody – call it what you will – this beautiful bird is probably my favourite of all, and I still cannot fathom out why so many shots regard it as being in any way second class. The head, neck and tail are predominantly grey, apart from the black tip on the tail and the green, white and purple patch that you see on the side of the adult's neck. The back and wings tend to be grey with perhaps a tinge of brown and a white wing patch. The breast also tends to be grey, but there is a sort of sheen of purple that is quite distinctive. The woodpigeon really is the prettiest of birds. It is also the largest of all our pigeons and doves, measuring about sixteen inches. I once weighed a really huge pigeon that I shot on a pea crop, and it weighed nearly two pounds, which I suspect is about maximum for Great Britain at least.

The sexes are pretty much alike, though I believe there is a slight difference in head shape, between male and female. The female builds a platform of twigs, usually in a tree but sometimes in ivy, on a building ledge, or in a bush or hedge very low to the ground. Pigeons lay during the spring, and the young hatch out towards the end

Pigeons will lay in the strangest of places – a stepladder left up against a gutter.

DOVES AND PIGEONS

Heavy bodies, broad and pointed wings, angled at the wrist giving them fast, direct flight.

STOCK DOVE

Grey, with two short black bars on each wing and a black tip on tail; often in flocks.

FERAL PIGEON

Plumage variable, often with broad black bars on the wings and white rump; often in towns.

WOODPIGEON

Grey, broad white wing-patches and white neck patch; fast direct flight; often seen in flocks.

COLLARED DOVE

Slim, pale grey below; long tail with white and black beneath; fast, direct flight.

TURTLE DOVE

Slim; long tail with white band at end; rapid flight with flicking wing-beats.

ROCK DOVE

Grey, with back lighter than head and underparts; two black bars on each wing; white rump.

A pigeon in flight.

of the summer. They are fed by both sexes with milk from their crop. I love watching pigeons courting – especially males. They have an up-and-down sort of flight, and you can hear their wings flapping as they fly up. That's a beautiful sound that I always associate with those lovely warm days of summer. Sometimes, you can see them courting on the ground as well, and that gives rise to all manner of strange movements with lots of bowing and mutual caressing with the bill. I've even seen the male feed the female in some sort of ritual.

Sadly, it's the feeding habits of this bird that make it the target it is. There's no doubt that the pigeon is one of agriculture's worst pests, and it is impossible to overestimate the damage it does all the year round. The pigeon will eat almost

everything that the farmers sow, and it is a great opportunist. Pigeons just seem to know unerringly where food is available. As a boy, I was told an old tale about a hailstorm – apparently one of the most fearsome that ever came to the Eastern Counties. It took a line south to north about two or three miles in width and mercilessly destroyed cereal crops, levelling them to the ground and scattering the grain inches deep in the fields. Pigeons flocked to the scene in immense numbers. It seems tens of thousands of the birds arrived literally within hours, and guns from all parts made for the scene, shooting them with the blunderbuss weapons they had in those days. A lot of birds were killed with each shot, but it didn't seem to make any difference to the numbers on the ground and in the air. I know that's

A pair of pigeons rubbing beaks in a springtime courting ritual.

an extreme case, but it does illustrate how there is a system of communication between birds that draws them to the most abundant feeding spots.

During the winter and spring pigeons feed on any green plants coming up and pick them so close to the earth that they weaken them. The pea crop is probably the favourite pigeon food, but they'll feed on newly sown grain in spring or the ripening crop, staying on the stubble field in the autumn. They love turnip crops and will gorge on sugarbeet leaves, especially when the weather is hot and dry. Fields of Brussels sprouts can be stripped bare. They absolutely adore oilseed rape and will gorge on it day-in day-out given half a chance. In fact, nothing is safe, and I've even found small, marble-sized potatoes in their crops at times. They'll eat all sorts of berries and even soft fruit from walled gardens if they can get it: berries from ivy trees, rowan bushes, cherries from the orchard and dockleaves. Wherever there is food, pigeons will find it. Nevertheless, I've drawn up a list of the major pigeon foods during specific seasons which I think will be of use when you are looking round for shooting grounds.

A hide in a field of linseed.

From April to June, cereal sowings, peas and beans, clover and weed seeds and leaves, tree buds and flowers, young pea shoots and leaves, pansies and chickweed all go down well. From July to September, pigeons gorge on ripe, or at least partly ripe, grain and any grain in the stubble. Peas take over as favourite, along with beans and clover and especially oilseed rape. Moving into October and December you'll find them feeding on the drilled winter cereals, still taking clover and weed seeds, gorging on acorns and hawthorn berries. Clover still figures from January to March, and so do blue lucerne leaves and also oilseed rape leaves along with the grain from any old stubble that's left over. Sheep turnips and kale are popular, as are ivy berries. As soon as the cereals are sown in March, the pigeons will be on that as well. If you find any of these you can be quite sure that pigeons won't be far away for too long.

POPULATION AND DISTRIBUTION

The number of pigeons in this country has always caused controversy – at least for a century or so. As a boy, I was told that the number of pigeons had risen in the previous century because the woods were better keepered, certainly in the shooting counties. Their predators – sparrowhawks especially – were kept down, and as a result the number of pigeons rose alarmingly. I suppose this trend continued and even accelerated in the 1960s when pesticides began to have the same or an even worse effect on the hawk population.

However, the woodpigeon population is not without problems of its own, and really bad weather such as that of 1962–63, will have a dramatic effect on the bird, I can tell you. Once food becomes scarce, pigeons either have to leave for pastures new or stay and suffer the

Very cold weather, such as this, causes great problems for the pigeon which cannot dig for its food.

A fantail pigeon surveys the garden scene.

consequences. There is also the effect of shooting to consider. The British Association for Shooting and Conservation (BASC) says many thousands of its members shoot woodpigeons each year, but the real number, taken nationwide, will be far higher than that, I am quite sure, and my own guess is that the number is probably nearer 300,000 and rising. On top of that, you've got to add the casual element: people who shoot only from time to time. That's a lot of people popping away at the flocks, especially when you consider some are very keen indeed.

The sport is certainly getting very organized. The National Pigeon and Pest Control group, based in Yorkshire, contacts farmers who are having problems with pigeons and then gives out the shooting details to a growing number of pigeon shooters. The idea is that the farmer gets rid of some pigeons, and the sportsman gets a variety of cheap sport. It obviously works very well, especially in the more northerly counties where there is less organized shooting in the woods, and syndicates are not quite as powerful. The organization now has a great deal of shooting in the North and Midlands as far south as Northampton and Bedford. I have a feeling that it will spread into East Anglia as well before long.

Money, sadly, rears its ugly head in pigeon shooting, not just from the farmers' point of view but also in the calculations of some of the shooters. I have always been a little bit worried about the number of pigeons we export from Britain. In fact, this has long been an issue, and twenty years ago the great Archie Coates estimated that 2½ million pigeons were going to the continent each year. There is no doubt that this is still happening. The French – I have to admit with some reluctance – are a lot more adventurous in their eating habits than the British, and it seems the French housewife is quite keen to buy the odd pigeon or two each week or month. As the price paid is quite high, there is a strong incentive to sell on the Continent and not in Britain where pigeons are virtually given away.

A population figure of 10 million birds for Great Britain has often been bandied about, but how this figure is calculated beats me. I feel the same way about the tradition that there is an autumn and winter migration into the country. Perhaps to an extent there is and perhaps we see some pigeons come down from the north if the weather gets very cold, but I firmly believe my own pigeons don't move a great deal unless they have to. They might fly around the county looking for food, but I'm not sure about them heading off for West Africa, as I've read they do.

Pigeon shooting has remained much the same over the last century, but it looks as though the European Union (EU) might force a close-season upon us some time. I don't like taking orders from London, never mind from even farther afield, I'll tell you. However, the threat has prompted new research into pigeons by the BASC working with the Game Conservancy and the National Farmers Union (NFU). This could be important, as we don't know a great deal about pigeons on a national scale, and I've got to admit that all knowledge is a good thing. Years ago, Archie Coates was talking about a decline in the pigeon population, and although I'm not sure about that these days, we must keep an eye on things as best we can.

4 THE PIGEON'S WORLD

In order to be a successful pigeon shooter, you have to understand the bird. It's the same with any type of shooting, and there are a few things that can have a real impact on pigeons and hence upon the pigeon shooter.

WEATHER CONDITIONS

The weather has a considerable effect on the way pigeons behave. First consider the effects of heavy rain: like all birds, pigeons are very susceptible to pouring rain, and if you stop to think about it, you will realize that you don't see many birds – of any sort – in the air when it is wet. Thus, if you're in two minds about whether or not to go out, and heavy rain has been forecast, you would probably be wise to stay in bed and wait for the next day, which might be a good deal drier.

I remember remarking all the way through the autumn and winter of 1993–94 that there were hardly any big pigeon flocks to be seen at all, and that was a period when it rained virtually all day every day, and we had floods month after month. You see, what I think happens is that the pigeons wake up in the morning, see the rain and simply don't fancy it. However, they have to feed on something, so they reluctantly accept the elements and get out of their leafy beds eventually. Pigeons are like sheep, and if a few get out, then a few more will join them, and then a few more, and then others, and so on until they're all out feeding in a big flock.

Of course, there's more to this than just the birds feeling depressed. When the weather is really bad, the fields become like porridge, and the farmers can't get out. This means that they're not ploughing or drilling, and everything comes

A storm might well bring pigeons in from the continent.

to something of a standstill. If the rain is cold, the crops won't be growing either, so there's really nothing much for the pigeons to go out and harvest. It needs a bit of dry to get the farmers out and start things rolling all over again.

Most of us go out pigeon shooting at least half the time to rid the farmer of vermin, but assuming that you like to eat the pigeons you shoot, this would be a bad time to go out anyway because they really do lose condition very quickly. You will find that after long periods of hard weather their breasts are like razor-blades and the poor things haven't got any meat on them at all.

Ideal conditions are when the rain goes, the weather warms up, the ground dries out and the crops go in. Then the pigeons will band up and begin to pile on weight. Their crops will be full and there'll be plenty of meat on them, so you can get out there and do the farmer a real service, knowing that the birds aren't eating just a few ivy berries or odd patches of clover left on the pastures.

You'll find that pigeons are susceptible to very hot, dry conditions, when the crops dwindle and shrivel up. We had a few summers like that in the early 1990s, when the pigeon population suffered. While pigeons will always know where to go to a pond or a stream to find water, you will also see them taking leaves off the crops to get some moisture. In fact, they probably depend on the leaves themselves for most of their water, and this can prove difficult in prolonged droughts.

Still, they much prefer those conditions to freezing temperatures. The worst occurrence for a pigeon is a wind frost that blasts the plant right through so that it becomes like iron. The poor birds have still got to feed, of course, and they will pick at vegetation like this, at anything that looks at all green and in any way accessible to them. They might be able to find a bit of kale or winter corn poking through the ground, but you will often find that their crop will be full of food that is actually frozen, even though it is inside the bird. I suppose this type of stuff fills the belly, but it can't be doing the poor creatures much good.

Let's say that you have a period of wind frosts and then snow begins to come in and covers the iron-like earth with a blanket of white. At times like this, you'll find the pigeon flocks have to fly miles and miles each day to search out their food sources. I know this sounds unkind, but you will often find that these are the very best conditions for decoying pigeons. Anything that is edible has to be targeted by the birds, so if you know of a crop that is visible and edible, you can just about guarantee that it will be visited day after day by many of the pigeons in the area. Of course you've got to remember that after a few weeks of weather like this, the pigeons might be bad for the pot, but you will still be getting rid of a pest.

Hungry as the birds are at times like this, don't assume that they will have lost all their caution. I remember once, when there was a three-acre strip of kale left in a field and a bale hide put at the end of a strip by a straw stack. My companions and I thought that the hide and the stack would merge together, and the pigeons wouldn't be suspicious. We were wrong. The hide worked to an extent but not really very well, even though the wind was in the right direction, and we had put a lot of decoys around the kale to try and get the pigeons in. We just couldn't really get them to come in to the stack. Maybe we were thinking too much of our own comforts when we set up our hide beside a straw-stack.

In really cold weather the big flocks appear.

Decoys occupy hedgerow and treetops to attract visiting birds.

Pigeons will also feed on kale, sprouts and maize in these conditions.

Pigeons feeding on snow-covered cabbage.

In the end, we built a bale hide actually in the kale itself. We draped the bales over and over with nets and then decorated those nets with sprigs of kale stuck in all around us. We obviously did the right thing because we had a very good day indeed. A friend of mine got in, and after he'd shot a fair bit I took over. I suppose we had seventy or eighty pigeons between us in less than three hours.

Another natural element that the pigeon shooter must consider is wind. Remember that whenever possible, birds will come in to land against the wind because it helps them control their landing manoeuvres. It doesn't matter how strong the wind is, the pigeon will land against it and use the wind with its wings and tail to effect a nice landing. A pigeon finds it very hard indeed to land with the wind behind, especially if it's of any strength. I've actually seen birds trying to do this in desperate situations and be tumbled over by the wind.

The stronger the head wind the better, and there are times when pigeons will come down and look almost as though they're stopping in mid-air and then just tumble to the ground – dropping, not really landing at all in the normal sense. It's a dramatic sight, and you'll really learn to appreciate the birds that you're out to shoot.

The wind has to become very strong indeed before it causes pigeons any concern at all. Sometimes what happens is that a gale springs up in the night when the pigeons are at roost. Obviously, if the trees begin to sway a bit, the pigeons are likely to get knocked about, and they will clear off, leaving the trees altogether. Next morning you'll find them scattered about, sitting all over the place and probably pretty tired and shaken as well. They'll probably wait until the wind dies down a fair bit before flocking up again and beginning to feed hard once again.

NATURAL PREDATORS

Of course, it isn't just the weather that causes pigeons problems, or we characters underneath with guns; they do have natural predators, especially birds of prey. Of those, probably the worst threat is the sparrowhawk, although I have seen kestrels tackle pigeons in the past. Pigeons really are terrified of big hawks on their patch, and you'll see them do the most dramatic things to get away. For example, when you're roost shooting, it is common to see pigeons sitting out in trees in the park or the fields, just looking at the wood before deciding whether or not to go in and roost. They'll do this all the more if they suspect that somebody is in there with a gun. They want to come in, but they are being wary, taking their time. You'll see them if you've got binoculars. If you scan the skyline, you will see them huddled in the trees, probably looking in your direction. Then you'll see them all rise up and dive away in a big cloud. What has happened is that a sparrowhawk has come their way looking for a meal before bedtime.

The sparrowhawk is one of the pigeons' deadly enemies.

Profile of a fox – deadly predator of any pigeon resting near the ground.

I remember once an osprey wandered in a couple of miles from the coast and was spending a few days fishing, for carp I suppose, on one of the local lakes. Anyway, I remember seeing the osprey flying along the woodland belt towards James' Wood and about three or four hundred yards in front of it the pigeons were rising up and disappearing in clouds. They were probably absolutely terrified of the bird, and even when it had gone past, they were still wary of going back into the wood. Pigeons have remarkable eyesight and they put it to good use, searching for the glint of a gun, as well as the sun on the beak of a sparrowhawk!

Foxes and badgers are also natural predators. They will take any wounded or sick bird or even one that's been knocked off its perch in the night.

However, they are by and large restricted to the ground and can't do a great deal of harm to healthy birds in the trees.

I really enjoy just sitting in the wood, looking up and absorbing the pigeon's world. There's much to notice, and it's all bound to help you. For example, you might hear a jay begin to call, then some blackbirds mobbing it and chasing it off. That jay may then fly on a bit until it finds a pigeon's nest and raid it. In fact, pigeons will lay two or three times a year if they lose their clutch, which I think happens quite a lot. You could not have a more flimsy nest than that of the pigeon – just a little scoop of a few sticks – and so the eggs and the chicks really stand out. Up there, pigeons have a lot of enemies: jays, magpies, squirrels, stoats, crows, rooks, jackdaws, owls and hawks.

One of the pigeons' predators.

It's fortunate for the pigeon that it's such an adaptable sort of character that knows its way around the countryside as well as it does. Pigeons can make use of all sorts of little things that come their way. Only the other day, my neighbour was cutting his grass for the first time of the year, and I noticed that pigeons were sitting on the fence watching him. What they did then was go down and take bits of clover that he'd cut. Talk about opportunists!

A lot of sheep have just been let out into the park, and pigeons follow them around day after day. What I think is happening there is that when the sheep eat they pull up the turf and expose all sorts of hidden seeds, so the pigeons are really making merry following these woolly providers. It's no coincidence, and I've watched them day after day, week after week.

I really hope you learn that there's more to pigeons than simply shooting them and that you can derive a great deal of fun and satisfaction from watching them and building up a vision of pigeons and their world. The real pigeon shooter is something of a naturalist, and you will only become one of those with constant observation and a great deal of affection for the wild world of nature.

5 THE IMPORTANCE OF CROPS

The whole purpose of pigeon shooting is to rid the countryside of a really troublesome pest: ask any farmer and he'll tell you that pigeons do more harm than anything else to his crop. One of the big problems is that pigeons have such broad tastes.

They do not like any one thing in particular; if they did, life would be easier for the farming community. In fact, pigeons will tire of anything, no matter how big a delicacy it is for them. Suddenly, for no apparent reason, the flocks will be up and off,

Dawn in early winter and the pigeon will be looking for breakfast.

Pigeons love feeding on the stubble fields.

looking for something fresh. I suppose they're just like us, and they get bored with eating the same sort of thing and need a change.

It's important that the successful pigeon shooter recognizes this behaviour and keeps a sharp eye on all the fields in his vicinity. As soon as pigeons really begin to look interested in a field, you need to get down there fast and do the business before they decide to up and off, and you've got to find them again. In my pigeon shooting career, there stick out several occasions when I've really scored through keeping my eye very closely on the crops around.

Peas are a real attraction for pigeons, and even though they're dressed with pink or blue powder when they're drilled, that doesn't seem to put pigeons off. They still eat with gusto. I don't know if the powder killed any of them at first, and they built up an immunity, but certainly it doesn't seem to bother them these days.

I remember one particular day when peas had just gone in, and the next day I saw pigeons flocking there in numbers. It was quite a big field, and I got into a hide at one side near a wood, whilst my friend Charlie moved in at the other by a hedgerow. We were there for only two hours early in the morning, and by the end I had shot ninety pigeons and Charlie had taken another sixty. That was a hundred and fifty in just two hours from a field of freshly drilled peas: just imagine the damage that the birds were doing and how much more damage they'd have carried on doing if they had been left alone. This year I have noticed that some farmers have drilled their peas a bit deeper, and the pigeons seem to have got the message!

Newly drilled barley is almost as big a draw as peas. I vividly remember walking along Waterloo Wood one evening and seeing the pigeons in the trees there in huge flocks. The wood was absolutely bursting with pigeons, believe me, and when I got home I rang the farmer out of curiosity to see what he'd put in the field. It was barley, and when I told him about the pigeons, he pleaded with me to do something about them.

Always one to oblige, I got up early the next morning and just as I had guessed the field was grey with birds. I'd put up just a little hide in the hope of getting permission and slid in there. The wind was perfect, and I did not need to put many decoys out at all so thick were the pigeons in the area. To cut the story short, I guess I had well over a hundred pigeons in just two or three hours. I never bothered to count them, and certainly couldn't have counted them at the time as the shooting was so brisk. However, it needed two journeys to carry all the pigeons back to the car, and I reckon that I can take sixty or so in one go with the gear so I've always settled on a figure of above a hundred in my own mind.

After such a good morning, I decided that I'd better go again, and the next day two of us went. However, there was no shooting at all. Obviously I had done a really good job on just that first day. We saw the odd straggler, but that was it. I had hit the pigeons really hard and moved them on to a place where they had more confidence, and the farmer was very, very pleased with me. In fact, that morning my friend and I got a vehicle and had a good drive round till we found that great big pigeon flock. The following day we managed to get in there and shoot more of them, and they actually left the area for a good while. That's the key: look for the crops, look for the pigeons, hit them hard, get them on the move out of the area and all the farmers will be pleased with you.

FINDING SPORT

There are all sorts of things that you can do to find sport. For example, in very hard weather, flocks tend to gather together, and you will find an enormous number of birds as they struggle to make ends meet. When the land freezes over, it is hard for a bird that doesn't scrap but rather pulls food with its beak. This makes kale a very useful food for the birds when temperatures drop very low.

Temperatures have never gone down much further than they did in 1963! I remember that desperate winter very well, especially one night when I was in the pub, talking to one of the farm managers. Apparently a lot of pigeons had got on to a field of kale that was being cut for the cattle, and I was asked to help. I gladly agreed.

The day dawned absolutely freezing, and there had been a heavy snow fall overnight. I got to the field and found a lot of kale laid out in rows for the cattle as I'd been told, but there was a lot still standing with a tremendous covering of snow. What I did was walk into this kale with a fork and knock all the snow off the tops about twenty yards in front of a hide that I had put up. This obviously exposed the green, which stood out like a beacon in amongst the sea of white. The trick worked a treat, and once the birds came back they swooped down to the kale that I had exposed (I'd also put in a few decoys on the top of the kale just to encourage them). The green of the kale and the few swinging decoys gave me a tremendous day's shooting and earned a great deal of praise from the farm.

Linseed is a favourite pigeon crop. I once had a part-time job keeping down rabbits and pigeons

Will Garfit with an impressive bag.

Birds feed on linseed and rape as soon as the plants are visible.

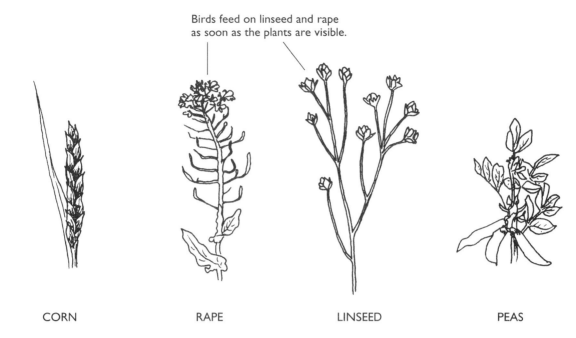

CORN RAPE LINSEED PEAS

A few popular crops.

An early example of the gunmaker's art.

on The Heath, where there were ninety acres or so sown with linseed. I'd put up four large bale hides around the field ready for the pigeon attack: two in the middle of the field and one at each end, so positioned that I felt most of the area could be covered. I knew the linseed would attract a lot of pigeons because it also happened to be right in the middle of one of the flight paths. Everything pointed to a bonanza.

I had an acquaintance who had been pestering me to let him have a bit of shooting, so I put him on the field first, as soon as I heard pigeons had found it and were beginning to feed there. He phoned me to say that he'd had a good day, and that evening I went to the field to see where he'd

been shooting. It was obvious which hide he'd been in because there were cartridge cases everywhere (something I really do not like to see, as it is important to clean up after you have been shooting). I made a mental note of this and promised to tell the man what I thought of it when I next saw him.

I decided to stick with that hide for the next day, one of those right in the middle of the field. I moved in while it was still dark, and as soon as light broke the pigeons came in swarms. For at least half an hour it was bedlam, but then there was a lull. I was about to pack up and move on when flocks of pigeons began to reappear – really huge ones on a regular basis.

Wind direction – from behind bale hide.

Wind damaged areas in field where pigeons land.

Wind damaged crops.

The pigeon will feed everywhere – even on a newly cut lawn.

There was an air display taking place about three miles away, and the various aeroplanes, helicopters and so on were driving the pigeons wild. They were flying around in flocks, disturbed by the aircraft, seeing my decoys and a tempting looking linseed field and they were coming down in droves. I took almost a hundred pigeons in two hours.

The interesting thing was that, around lunch time, I left all the decoys out and went off to find my brother-in-law who I know loves pigeon shooting. We got back in the afternoon and stayed a good while: all we managed to shoot were nine birds. It was much the same the next day when I was there for a good while and got just thirty. After that, the linseed was left pretty well alone, even though the crop was tempting and the flight path went right over it. Pigeons just knew that those bale hides meant a lot of trouble to them, and kept away. There were still plenty of pigeons in the area, for if you've shot a hundred birds, then you can be quite sure that you've probably seen a thousand or so. It is just a good example of how pigeons begin to recognize danger and will go off to look for fields anew, always trying to keep one step ahead of you. For that reason you have got to keep as close an eye as you possibly can on the land around you and listen to anybody who might have information that will help you out.

6 FLIGHT PATHS

Pigeons flocking in to feed in hard weather. There are times when they just keep coming no matter how many are shot.

Flight paths are a topic of debate among pigeon shooters. Some doubt whether they exist at all. Ask any countryman, though, and he'll tell you straight. Day after day, week after week, year after year, the man who really knows the locality like the back of his hand will be aware that pigeons constantly use the same route to get around the countryside. This is not imagination: flight paths exist as surely as I do!

When I refer to flight paths I don't mean a route that a flock of pigeons uses from time to time from a roost to a particular field. (They might actually take this direction a few times until they get fed up with a particular crop and move on, but you won't see them taking that way again for some time, if ever.) Flight paths are much more permanent.

In fact, when I was a boy I was told of a flight path over the heath, which stretched for several miles across open countryside, avoiding villages, and took in various pieces of woodland as well as a number of farms. That was some forty years ago, and believe you me most of the pigeons in the area use that very same path to this day. They'll even use it when the wind isn't totally right for them. They fly across it to stay with the route they know so well. Naturally, you won't find all pigeons using the flight path all of the time: if you did there would be one huge flock of pigeons moving around like a cloud of locusts! Rather, what you'll find is groups of pigeons using the flight path around their patch then turning off it here or there to get to a particular roost or feeding ground.

Good pigeon shooters should be aware of flight paths. If you find a crop or roost that pigeons are using at a particular time, and it is close to a flight path, then it is much more likely to be patronized by the birds for a length of time. You see, pigeons are notoriously fickle. They might gorge on a single crop for a few days, and suddenly disappear, and it might be some time before another group

The farmer will try everything to keep the pigeon off his crops.

takes up on the field. If, however, the crop is situated on or near a flight path, you will find that even if one group of pigeons gets fed up with it, another will be ready to come in and take its place, and so you can put up a hide in the sure knowledge that a steady stream of pigeons – albeit different ones – will be using the field for a good time to come. This, believe me, is a real bonus. However, if you see pigeons on a crop like this, don't leave it for too long and don't assume that they will necessarily be there for a number of weeks: they can be off just as quickly as they came.

I should note here that pigeons will be really single-minded about a food source for a number of days and will think about nothing else. If, for example, they find a field of rape that they are very keen on, a flock of pigeons will stay there for days – even though it may well be a good way from a flight path. When they've finished feeding for the day, they will probably look round for a nearby wood to go and roost in rather than moving many miles back to a flight path and travelling unnecessarily. Thus, if you can't get out and build a hide and shoot the pigeons during the day, you might well be able to tuck yourself into the nearest convenient wood and shoot them as they're coming in to sleep.

There are one or two ways of cheating a little bit to make sure that your hide is going to be a success. I think 'cheating' is too strong a word, actually; it's more like trying to make that extra little bit sure that all the time and effort that you put in is not wasted. What I'm talking about is a very common sight in the autumn, particularly when flocks of pigeons are feeding on wheat stubble. If a field of wheat stubble is close to a flight path, you will tend to find that pigeons visit it for weeks at a time and that it is a constant draw. The problem is, especially if it's a big field, knowing where exactly the pigeons will feed each morning.

You can help them out a little bit on this by feeding up a small area for them close to where you want to put the hide. Say you have decided on your position for your hide, then build it and leave it for a short time while you put a pail or so of wheat down each day for incoming pigeons. Restrict the area that you feed to the sort of size of piece of ground that you would put decoys over. You can even mark it off if you like with a couple of big flints or bricks. You can probably get a few odd pails of wheat from the farmer, either free or very cheap indeed because he knows that you are doing him a favour in the long run.

A pail of wheat each day or so should do the job, and after a few feeds like this the pigeons will know that your particular piece of ground is always very rich in food, and many of them will flock there before visiting any other piece of the field. Of course, they will also get used to the hide, and after a few days of this, it will be easy for you to slip in early one morning with the scene set for a good day's sport.

Before I finish on flight paths, I would like to point out that many wild creatures have an incredible grasp of geography – something that humans probably can't begin to understand. You've only got to think of the amazing journeys birds and other animals take during the migration periods to be astonished. Think, too, of racing pigeons that seem instinctively to know their way around the countryside, or messenger pigeons. They're really extraordinary birds, there's no doubt about that, but then many animals have this same instinct. For example, you will find that badgers have well-worn tracks, or trods, that they use night after night all the way through the year as they plod around woods and meadows. In just the same way, you'll find that herds of wild deer will always cross streams or ditches at recognized points. The other night I was talking to a fisherman about this very subject, and he told me there was such a thing as a 'bream patrol route'. Apparently, these fish – considered pretty stupid by some anglers – virtually always move round big waters along certain well known routes. It seems that you can see them rolling every evening and early morning in exactly the same places at pretty much the same times, and the wise angler will bait up where he knows they're going to be passing. This type of ambush is very successful indeed for a bream shoal, and it seems similar to everything I've been saying about pigeons and their flight paths. In sum, ignore pigeon flight paths at your peril!

Pigeons and doves hold a special place in the countryside, not least for their tastiness on the plate.

7 THE WELCOMED PIGEON SHOOTER

It's important that all pigeon shooters remember that they are guests – invited guests perhaps, doing a good job, but guests all the same – and they have to show proper regard for every farmer's property where they find their sport. With that in mind, I would like to take a look at some of the things that we all should consider while enjoying a day's shooting.

First, it is desperately important to be very careful with your vehicle. Keep exactly where you're told to go, and don't drive over any fields where crops are being grown or even on rides

The bag and equipment needed to make it.

through woodland unless you have been given permission. Don't take any risks with marshy pieces of ground, and park where you know your vehicle is going to be safe. Just try asking the farmer for a tow out of mud at eight o'clock on a January night and see how unpopular you are!

Don't think that just because you have a four-wheel-drive vehicle it gives you the licence to go anywhere you want. Some are better than others and even they can get stuck. Even if the vehicle gets out, the ruts it will leave behind can really mess up a carefully prepared piece of ground for months afterwards. Believe me, your reappearance will not be welcome if you have totally churned up a carefully tended ride. I know that four-wheel-drive vehicles are very much a modern-day trend, but sometimes farmers really curse them. After all, most of us are lucky enough to have use of our legs, and we don't need to drive everywhere our fancy takes us.

Make sure that you park your vehicle carefully and thoughtfully too. Never cause an obstruction to fields or barns. There is nothing more infuriating for a busy farmer than finding he can't get into a field and having to trek around looking for you to move your vehicle out of his way. If you are not a regular in the area, it is not a bad idea to leave a note saying who you are, where you are and what you are doing, so that the farmer or keeper is quite sure there isn't an intruder about.

When you come to a gate, see if there's a stile nearby that you can climb over rather than attacking the gate itself. If you've got to climb over the gate, make sure that you climb on the hinge side rather than in the middle. Otherwise, the gate will gradually sag over the years and have to be re-hung. Obviously, if the gate can be opened, go through that way, but do make sure that you close it very firmly after you. I'm afraid that every now and again – twice to be exact – I've inadvertently left a gate open and cattle have got out into a field where they shouldn't have been. On each occasion I felt absolutely terrible, and checked and re-checked gates thereafter for the next ten or fifteen years!

Remember that just because a farmer has invited you on to a particular piece of land to shoot

pests for him, he has not given you the green light to make his farm your own. Don't wander anywhere your fancy chooses because there might be areas that the farmer is keeping as a sanctuary for some reason. It is also a courtesy to your host if you keep your eyes open and make sure that unwelcome visitors are not present on the land that you can see. This is especially the case if you are close to a pheasant wood where poachers might be attracted. If you see anything suspicious, make a note, writing down any car numbers, and inform the farmer later on.

Never shoot in the vicinity of any stock or other animals. Horses are especially nervous of gunfire, and if they bolt they can injure themselves badly. Only shoot over the crops to be protected, not at random wherever your fancy chooses. Remember that you are there primarily to do a service and not simply to satisfy your own shooting and sporting interests. If you're shooting over a crop that hasn't been harvested, then do be very careful not to harm it in any way when you're laying out your decoy pattern or collecting up the dead birds. You'll be surprised how much damage two or three pigeons shooters can do to the fringes of a field if they're not careful.

Be cautious with dogs. A lot of pigeon shooters like to take dogs with them for good reason, but some farmers object. Check up before you take a dog out with you for the day, especially when sheep or wildfowl are around. If you are in any doubt, ask, and don't take any risks with a dog that could cause upset later on.

Do not harm trees, bushes or hedgerows in any way at all when building your hides. For all you know, the farmer might have been tending that particular area for many years, and he won't appreciate it at all if he comes along and finds you've done a savage hatchet job on it. Do not leave empty cartridges lying about, as it advertises the fact that some pigeon shooters are messy creatures and something of a disgrace to the sport. Equally, don't leave any litter of any description behind you.

I think it's important to stress that you should shoot only pigeons when you are invited on to the land. You must not take a passing duck or even

The grim sight of a keeper on top of his job.

worse a pheasant or partridge under any circum-
stances, unless the farmer has expressly said you
can. You shouldn't even shoot a fox, unless you
know the farmer wants them thinned out. Obviously, there will be the odd occasion when you
make a mistake, but that's all you should ever do.
Never risk your arm by having a pop at something outside your jurisdiction.

As yet, there is no close-season for pigeon
shooting in Great Britain, but do be very careful
in the woods towards the beginning of the pheas-

ant season. Even if you have *carte blanche* on a
farm, always check with the farmer or keeper in
September and October as they may not want the
woods disturbed in what is a very sensitive time
in the shooting year.

In short, I think it's fair to say that you should
behave just as you would expect any guest to in
your own garden. If you are in any doubt about
anything, check up before you do something that
might anger your host and might jeopardize your
chances of further shooting.

8 THE PIGEON GUN

You can shoot pigeon with an air rifle, but the weapon of choice for pigeon shooters is the shotgun. Shotguns have been part of the English shooting scene for generations, and they have progressed quite a long way. We are very lucky that guns are so efficient today. For example, we take for granted breech-loading and automatic ejection of cartridges, which would have amazed pigeon shooters years back. Nowadays, the gun is an absolute treasure to handle, to possess and above all to use. Remember that, and make every effort to find a gun that suits you.

The keepers that used to teach me said, 'Find a gun that suits you because you'll never suit it, boy!' Trying to suit yourself to a gun will never work properly. Essentially, the stock of the gun

The older the gun, often the finer the engraving.

should nestle in the crook of your arm, allowing your finger to rest comfortably on the trigger. If you are longer in the arm, then you'll need a long stock, and if you're short, then a smaller one will be required. Try lifting the gun. It should swing into position without any fuss and you should feel perfectly at home with it. That's the key – it should fit you like a glove with no sweating or straining. You should feel as though it was made for you alone.

Once you have found a gun that you feel really suits you, see where the barrels are in relation to your master eye. With the gun into your shoulder, you shouldn't have to move your head too much. If you shoot from the right shoulder, your right eye is your master eye, and with the stock of the gun into your shoulder you should be able to look straight along the barrels without any problems at all. If you can't then you have the stock

moved to suit your individual build. You may even be able to find a gun with a stock that has a gentle cast-off, and you will find this much better than the one you are trying. If you are a well-built person with broad shoulders and you wear a lot of clothes when shooting in the winter (a time when we all tend to wrap up well against the elements), this is even more important. Then, and only then, might you need a bigger cast-off on your stock.

To see this cast-off on any shotgun all you have to do is stand the gun upright on the floor, holding the muzzle end of the barrels and the trigger pointed away from you. Hold the gun in this manner and take one step backwards without moving the stock of the gun on the floor. Lean the barrels towards you, look down the length of your shotgun and you will see that the stock of the gun falls away slightly: this is what

A weapon like this – over 200 years old – would have been loaded with pretty well anything considered lethal!

Everything should line up as easily as possible to the master eye.

The master eye looks up the barrel with total ease.

The gun should fit snugly in the crook of the arm.

we call the 'cast-off'. If you shoot from the right shoulder, the cast-off will be to the right as you look at it and vice versa if you shoot from the left shoulder. I do know people who have straight stocks who are perfectly good shots, but I do hope this consideration will help the novice to choose his gun properly.

The big danger for the new gun is that he hears that old Ted up the road has a gun for sale and goes and buys it from him cheap. It might be cheap, but it might also be useless for him. What's the point of saving a few pennies when you're starting out, only to find out later that you've made an expensive mistake? It is better to go to a gunsmith and try out a selection of guns so that you get exactly the right one. Believe me, it's a false economy to go out and buy the first gun you find.

Nowadays there is a lot of competition between gunsmiths and there are some bargains out there. You can pick up a good gun, brand new, fully guaranteed and totally safe, for between three and four hundred pounds. With that sort of money you can get a gun that will be a friend to you for all the days of your life.

GUN TYPE AND AMMUNITION

After comfort and ease with the weapon, there are several other considerations to bear in mind when it comes to making the final choice. For example, do you want a 'side-by-side' gun or an 'over-and-under' one? The traditional English sporting gun had the barrels placed side by side, and this lasted many people for most of their shooting lives. However, the modern trend is to go for one barrel under the other: the over and under. This has probably come about because of the growing interest in clay pigeon shooting. I don't know why, but clay pigeon shooters tend to prefer the over-and-under variety, and I suppose that number of people can't be wrong. However, I'm quite happy with my side-by-side, and I always have been. I know a great many successful pigeon shooters who are. It seems to me that anything else is just a fad.

You'll find that double-barrelled shotguns can be bought with a single-trigger mechanism or a double-trigger one. The choice is a matter of personal preference. Essentially, double-barrelled shotguns have a trigger to fire each barrel. The right-hand barrel, generally the one with the lightest choke and the one you'll use first, is fired with the front trigger, while the rear one fires the left barrel. This system does not suit everyone, however, there are those who prefer not to move their finger from one trigger to another when firing. The single-trigger gun was invented for just such people: the index finger – always the index finger – does not have to be moved at all. In addition, you needn't worry that your second barrel won't be ready for use immediately if you go for a single-trigger gun.

You also need to choose between a side-lock or a box-lock gun. Most people go for side-locks now because they're a little more streamlined. Then there is the choke and the bore to consider. These are complex decisions. Your gunsmith will advise you and help you decide what is best. There's always discussion about that because shooters are constantly looking for ways to get a bit of an advantage over each other – hoping a small detail will improve performance. I tell you, they'd be better off concentrating on their technique than worrying about technology.

The cost of a gun can rise steeply because of the type of wood the stock is made from and the carving on the body of the gun. You can easily pay a couple of hundred pounds extra (or thousands more if you're in that league!) for these features alone. A really good stock will be made out of walnut because it has beautiful gold, brown

and black markings. The markings are called the 'figure', and this often follows the grain of the wood, but it's not the same thing and you shouldn't get the two mixed up. Most people go for a really attractive, eye-catching figure on the stock and for that you'll be paying plenty of money, believe me. It's the same thing with the carving: the finer and more ornate it is, the more you'll have to pay. The choice, of course, is entirely up to you and your budget. What I would say is that if you're buying a gun that you want to last for a long time, make sure that you buy something that suits you first, and that you are proud of, second. You want that gun to be a friend for a very long time indeed – perhaps throughout your entire shooting life, so collect all the advice you can. After all, the better you know the gun, the better your shooting is likely to be. Don't forget that in the end it's your shooting technique and ability that is the crucial element when it comes to putting the pigeons down.

You will do very well indeed to think carefully about the type of ammunition that you choose for shooting pigeons. There are several points to consider when buying ammunition, and the last thing I want to do is make things too complicated, so I will try and keep the discussion as simple as I can.

Recently, many new guns seem to have come out and been made generally available. I think it's true to say that the 20-bore gun is very popular with younger people new to the sport. The reason is simple: the gun is nice and light, and you can still get the load of cartridge that you want. Being light, the gun is easy to carry and it's not uncomfortable to stand with for many hours when you're roost shooting, for example. The drawback to the 20-bore is that you get nowhere near as many shot in your pattern as you do with a 12-bore. This obviously makes the actual shooting that much harder. The 20-bore gun does have a pattern, of course, but it's smaller and tighter, and you're more likely to miss the bird. The 12-bore is a good all-rounder that most people would probably go for. It's a good standard gun, which is hard to better. The 16-bore is just a little lighter than the 12-bore, and

I suppose it is a half-way house between the two.

There are times when you can go lighter than the 20-bore. In my experience, this is generally when you find yourself shooting in young conifer woodland. If the trees are no more than twelve or fifteen years of age and about thirty feet high, you will find that a 410 shotgun is quite ample to kill birds in the top of the trees or even flying above.

Cleaning the gun is a vital task.

This is very light, satisfying shooting. The 410 is even smaller than the 20-bore with even less pellet-load and less pack and punch. The cartridges do differ in length, but providing the gun has been bored for such a cartridge, you can get 3-inch magnum cartridges that often prove excellent. However, it's got to be said that for the average pigeon shooter, the 410 is a rather specialized beast, and you would probably still be better looking at the 20-bore or 12-bore.

SHOT-PATTERN

A lot of consideration should go into the actual shot-pattern that your gun and cartridge produce. After all, it is the spread of the pellets in the air that is so crucial to bringing down the pigeon, and if the shot-pattern is irregular or unpredictable, then you will miss birds for no accountable reason, get frustrated and begin to question your own ability and technique.

Of course, an irregular shot-pattern could be the result of an old sub-standard gun. That is why it is important to go to a reputable dealer in the first place. Another cause of not killing the pigeon is using a cartridge that is too low-powered, especially in a wood with tall trees. There's no point in shooting at pigeons at height with an ounce-load of cartridge, because it just won't get there. In a nutshell, you've got to make sure that the ammunition has the strength that you need.

The average 12-bore cartridge will kill at thirty-five yards. If you've got ninety-foot trees, and the pigeons are twenty feet above that, you are obviously struggling, especially with a cheap cartridge. Like everything else in life, you get what you pay for.

If you think that you're not killing birds because your cartridge is just not up to the job, then move up a little bit. Spend a bit more money and you might find that you're on the right tracks again. You need to find out which size and make of cartridge suits your gun best. Once you have found out, stick to that make unless there is a really good reason for changing.

The best way of discovering which cartridge is exactly the best is by trial shooting. There are several ways of doing this, but a common and very practical method is to fire the gun at a target set up at a range of about fifteen yards. The best way of doing this is with what is called a Pattern Plate, and quite a few gun clubs around the country possess one. If at all possible, test your gun and its ammunition in the company of an experienced shooting instructor. He will often ask you to shoot a number of different targets from different positions before moving the Pattern Plate itself. The reason he does this is to build up your confidence and also to make sure that the gun you have fits you properly. By the time you have shot off a few cartridges, you should be feeling comfortable with your gun, and you can start the experiment.

An experienced instructor will probably get you to shoot from fifteen to twenty yards from the plate. At this distance, the shot-charge is pretty tight, so it's possible to locate the exact centre of the shot pattern. Several shots are taken at the mark on the plate, and a careful note is made of how and where each one strikes. Of course, the plate has to be repainted each time so the marks do not get confused. A tin of white emulsion paint and a brush are all you need. As soon as a shot-pattern has been recorded, simply paint over it with a good coating of emulsion, and you will find that it dries almost immediately outdoors – certainly fast enough to record the next shot-pattern.

Ideally – especially at as close as fifteen yards – you are looking to get a pretty tight shot-pattern. Of course it will spread out as you move farther away from the target. At thirty-five to forty yards, for example, you should still expect to deliver up to seventy per cent of the shot within a circle of about thirty inches in diameter. Once you are doing that, you can be pretty sure that your gun, cartridge and yourself are all fairly well suited, and if you are missing birds, it is not the fault of your tools! Happy shooting!

9 PIGEON SHOOTING TECHNIQUE

Let's start with gun safety, as it is the most important thing you'll ever have to learn as a pigeon shooter. There are, of course, some basics that you must never forget. Whenever you are carrying a gun make sure that it is open. That way everyone else around you can see that it is unloaded and safe. Never, ever, whatever you do, stand in a party of people with a closed gun. The others, whether they tell you or not, will be tense and possibly even scared. If you are armed and with someone who is not, make sure that person walks behind not beside or in front of you. Always remember that once a gun is loaded and closed and you have put the safety catch off, you have got a lethal weapon in your hands, so you cannot be too careful.

You need to learn to take care of yourself as well. If you are in your hide early in the morning and you're crouched down waiting for pigeons to come over, you must keep your gun open – loaded, but open. You can close it when the pigeons come over and you get up to have your shot. Remember that anything can happen in that small, cramped, often slippery hide of yours. Once you've got a closed gun in your hands with the safety catch off, you can never be quite sure that you're totally safe. After all, you could slip or side-step or trip over something and that would be that … dead as a pigeon!

It is true that modern guns are safer than the old ones used to be, and I do not want to make you absolutely paranoid. The old hammer-guns were real beasts, and I know of more than one man who's shot himself climbing over a fence or gate. I suppose seeing disasters like that has steadied me up and made me realize just how dangerous a gun is and how I must never underestimate it or let my concentration wander.

An excellent habit to adopt is always to check that you have unloaded your gun when you have finished shooting and when you put the gun into its sling. I even check again when I take the gun indoors before putting it in the cabinet.

It is important to clean your gun regularly and oil it as the makers recommend. If your gun is wet – and it often will be in the winter – don't put it back in the sling until it is well and truly dry. If you do, the sling will get wet and the gun will gradually rust, which is potentially dangerous. It is the law that guns be locked up in a cabinet with two five-lever locks on it. Position that cabinet away from everyone, out of sight, out of mind and somewhere it is as thief-proof as possible. Whatever you do, never leave your gun lying around the house, because anything could happen. Try to make sure that cartridges go in a separate cabinet if you can.

SHOOTING STYLE

Once you have grasped all the principles of safety around guns, you will be ready to establish your own shooting style. I personally like to keep the gun down until the last minute, but a different style of shooting has emerged lately largely because of the popularity of clay pigeon shooting. In that sport you put your gun to your shoulder, shout 'Pull', aim and squeeze the trigger, but it's different in the wild. You don't know when nature is going to send those real pigeons across for you to have a shot at. Therefore, you should walk with your gun open, see your pigeon, close your gun, bring it up, put the safety catch off, aim and squeeze the trigger, in that sequence. You are not using a rifle, but a shotgun, and there's no need to close either eye, so the whole thing can

The well-stocked gun room – weapons old and new – always kept well locked.

be done comparatively quickly. Of course, the routine I've just described is equally applicable if you're roost shooting or you're in a hide.

When you bring your gun up, it is vital that you swing through the bird that you're aiming for. Keep that swing going until you are aiming past the bird, then squeeze. Beginners tend to swing to the bird, then stop and squeeze, and that pigeon will be two or three feet away by the time the shot gets to it. Another thing to remember is to swing your barrels in from the direction that the bird is coming, whatever the route. In my mind, you don't just poke the gun out and then pull the trigger. You should move your gun in a gentle arc, following the flight of the bird. Imag-

ine that your gun is a long stick and that you're trying to swipe the pigeon out of the air with it. That should help you keep the barrel on the bird and keep it swinging, following its flight, so that when you squeeze you will be successful.

Of course, some pigeons fly slowly and some go like bullets, but to my mind that is the attraction of pigeon shooting. You just never know what sort of birds you'll be after on a particular day, and this is where experience and developing skill enters the equation. In fact, I know some guns, pretty good ones at that, who are brilliant with fast birds and much poorer with slow ones. They've never really been able to master the art of putting a slow pigeon down.

The author admires an 18th-century gun used for game and pigeons both.

A lot depends on the wind and the direction in which the pigeon is flying. Pigeons generally fly into the wind, but of course that can't happen all of the time, and sometimes you'll see a pigeon with the wind at its tail going like a rocket. Just swinging your gun past it won't be nearly good enough in such a situation, and you've got to give it a good lead before squeezing: I guess seven or eight feet would be about right. On the other hand, if you're tracking a slow bird, swing about four feet in front, and you should be in with a very good chance.

You need to learn to use your gun as skilfully as possible. Your gun will have two barrels in all probability, but these barrels will differ slightly. If you have an over-and-under gun, then the top barrel will be the choke barrel and the bottom one the improved, or cylinder, barrel. If you have a side-by-side gun, the left barrel will be the choke barrel and the right one the improved, or cylinder, barrel. What does that mean? In simple terms, the choke barrel will keep the shot-pattern

A pigeon comes in over stubble.

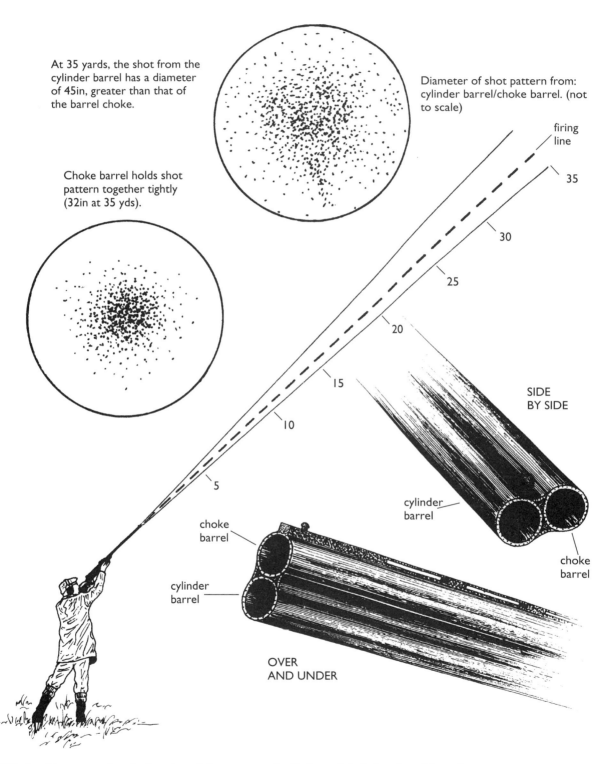

At 35 yards, the shot from the cylinder barrel has a diameter of 45in, greater than that of the barrel choke.

Choke barrel holds shot pattern together tightly (32in at 35 yds).

Diameter of shot pattern from: cylinder barrel/choke barrel. (not to scale)

firing line

35

30

25

20

15

10

5

SIDE BY SIDE

cylinder barrel

choke barrel

choke barrel

cylinder barrel

OVER AND UNDER

Side-by-side, over-and-under barrels and shot-patterns of cylinder and choke barrels at 35 yards.

The business end!

longer. The muzzle of the barrel is slightly cone-shaped inside, and this chokes the shot as it goes out into the air making sure it keeps its pattern over a far greater distance. In practice, when you're sitting in your hide, this means that if you see a pigeon at around thirty yards or more, then you go for it with the choke barrel because otherwise the shot will be so spread out by the time it reaches the bird it will probably sail through unscathed. Of course, it would be quite different if your pigeon was ambling along only twenty or twenty-five yards away. In that case, you would use the improved, or cylinder, barrel and the shot pattern would open up nicely to meet it.

There are no real tips that I can share about how to estimate how far away a pigeon is. You have to learn from experience, and after a while it will become instinctive. You'll have no hesitation in choosing which barrel to use.

WOUNDING BIRDS

The last thing any decent gun wants to do is wound a bird and not kill it. That's why your gun technique is so vital. If you're in your hide, have a pot at a bird, see it come down and then see it is wounded and walking, get out at once and kill it. You should always try to keep your eyes on a walking wounded bird. If you get out and can't see it at once, it has almost certainly moved into cover somewhere. Hedgerows are the obvious favourites or clumps of long grass. There used to be an old rogue, whose name I won't mention, who would leave the walking wounded, thinking that they would pull live pigeons in. Not only was he doing a bad thing, but to my mind they would be scaring new pigeons off. Walking wounded birds would be moving from the decoys, flapping their wings, and that could not look right at all.

10 DECOYS

Daybreak in foul winter weather.

Shooting pigeons over decoys, or 'deeks' as they are called sometimes, is probably the standard way to get a bag of these birds, and over the years the method has developed into a real art form, believe me. There is a great deal of skill involved in deciding what decoys to use, how to set them and where to put them.

Decoys work because pigeons are flock birds and get a great deal of confidence from feeding and sleeping in the company of others. When a pigeon flies over a field and sees decoys, it feels somehow encouraged to go down and join them. If they are feeding there so confidently, he reasons, things must be safe thereabouts. Poor bird!

What have we in here – a sack of deeks!

There's probably an element of greed in his thinking as well.

We know pigeons have brilliant eyesight – as sharp as a needle – and they can see decoys over a quarter of a mile away, but I still sometimes find it hard to understand how many birds will fly over so soon after you put your decoys down, even if they don't actually come to land. If you ask me, there's something like a sixth sense that travels along the airwaves. Of course, there is also the question of flight paths to bear in mind and the ability of the person setting the decoys to read the countryside correctly.

The big question is where to get your decoys in the first place. Many different types of shop-bought ones are available – often plastic and some-

times wood. Simply go around looking for the most realistic ones that you can find. I like life-size ones, the right colour with the dullest sheen possible. Anything shiny is right out. Have you ever seen shiny feathers, after all? It is always a problem when the weather alternates between showers and sunshine. The decoys get wet and when the sun comes out they glisten in a way that a real pigeon never would, giving the game away totally.

Taking all this into account, it is still a good idea to start out buying some artificials. How many is up to you and your pocket and also, to an extent, how far you can reckon on carrying them every time. If your fields are very remote, it can be a chore lugging great sackfuls across one wet meadow after the next, but there are times when a really big carpet of decoys is useful. If you can afford perhaps thirty to forty birds, all well and good. If not you can work up the numbers and keep adding to your 'flock' with good examples when you see them come along. I've got a first team of perhaps forty artificials in addition to dozens that have been relegated to the shed, and there are times when I use them all.

To my mind there is nothing to beat the dead birds themselves, set up as decoys. In fact, as I shoot over my artificials, I'll always take advantage of a lull to get out of the hide, pick up birds I've shot and set them up alongside the artificials. After a while, with any luck at all, I'll soon have all my artificials back in the sack and a whole flock of real ones out there doing the job for me.

SETTING UP

There are various ways of setting the real bird up as a decoy, but remember, real or artificial, the trick is to get everything looking as natural as possible. For that reason, in years gone by, tame pigeons were set out on the field to flap about and draw the wild ones in to be shot. It was not a pleasant practice at all, and I think we're all heartily glad that it isn't done nowadays.

I personally set my birds up the old way – on short sticks taken from the hedgerow and sharpened at both ends. Generally the sticks are about six to eight inches long. I put one end in the head – under the chin – and the other in the ground. Then push the pigeon down and clamp its wings

Hedgerow stick inserted into pigeon's neck.

A propped decoy.

A real bird supported by plastic coated wire.

P. Groombridge

A dead bird set up as a decoy.

firmly. It usually sits very nicely indeed and looks quite realistic. There are those who use cradles of plastic-coated wire these days. I suppose these last well, and you are saved the task of topping them up from the hedge when the wooden ones break, but I'm just a little bit concerned by the look of them myself. I suppose the thing is that I have confidence in what I've been taught to do and what I've been doing all my life, and it would be crazy to change a winning habit.

There are quite a few weird contraptions out now for mounting dead decoys so that they look as though they're flying or landing, and I admit some work quite well – much better than the old flapping decoys that used to be for sale. With those, you needed to pull the wings with string or wire to make the wings flap – hopeless! There were wires everywhere, and if you didn't trip over them, the dogs did, especially when you were trying to get back to the hide because you'd just seen a flock of birds coming your way! Even then, you'd spend so much time pulling wires that the birds would be in and you didn't even have a gun in your hand. The point is that artificial aids never make up for field craft: you simply can't buy success when it comes to pigeon shooting.

If I know I'm going out shooting again soon, I'll often save a few of the pigeons that I've shot

If you just wet the eye of the dead bird as you set it up, it will shine and look more life-like.

Setting up the real bird to draw in the others.

and put them straight in the freezer to use as decoys on the next trip. In my experience it's no good doing this unless the birds are really fresh. If you leave them for a few days they're not nearly as effective. First of all, you've got to wrap each bird in paper to prevent them from sticking to each other. Secondly, you should push the wings firmly together so that the bird will stiffen up as naturally as possible. It's then a simple task to take the dead pigeons from the freezer, unwrap them and place them out on the ground. It really couldn't be easier.

However, I don't just leave things there. When I set them up, I wet my thumb and rub it over the dead bird's eyes. I've found over the years that even this little bit of detail helps. You see, a dead eye sinks into the head and looks com-

pletely lifeless, but some moisture perks it up no end. If you watch live pigeons out in the crop, you will notice that a live bird will turn its head and look up when a new bird comes into land, so I think that the eye is a very important signal indeed. If a lot of dead eyes greet the live bird, he's bound to be suspicious. You can see now the sort of detail I believe is necessary with decoys. Don't take any chances at all: make your decoys as natural as you can.

This might involve a lot of fiddly work. For example, an old trick to make an artificial more realistic is to stick real wings to its sides. A few dabs of superglue and you've got a plastic decoy that looks more like the real thing and is therefore more likely to work, especially when there isn't much wind or the sun is out.

I always keep an eye on my decoys, artificials or dead birds, especially in the wind. If a few get blown over, your whole patch will look wrong, and you'll find that birds begin to turn away. It's much the same with birds that I've just shot. You can get away with a few lying about, especially if the wings are spread out. The others will think that they're landing and may come to inspect because they think there's food. However, don't rely on this. If there are dead birds everywhere in all sorts of positions, the fresh ones coming in will begin to show caution and perhaps not even come near.

Lofting Decoys

There is always some new craze in decoys. For example, there is something of a boom in using very large decoys, nearly twice the size of the natural bird. I suppose these giant woodies are very visible and initially might attract pigeons from great distances, but what do the birds think when they get close up and have a better look? I would certainly be very wary about putting these monsters anywhere but on the very edge of my set-up.

Another fad is to raise or 'loft' your decoys. This can prove a useful trick, especially if your hide is against a small tree or something similar, and a decoy in it will be visible from far away. You can even loft decoys in trees in a roosting wood, but you must allow plenty of time to get them up in the branches before the roost flight begins.

There are various ways of lofting decoys: you can climb a tree or throw ropes over. I've even seen it done with a bow and arrow! You can buy metal lofting poles to push the bird up high, but do be careful with overhead power cables, as you only get one chance at this sort of thing!

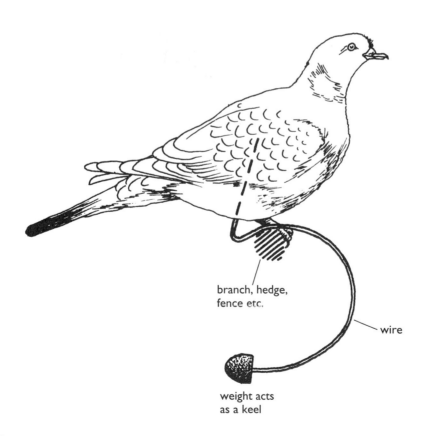

branch, hedge, fence etc.

wire

weight acts as a keel

Tree/hedgerow decoy support.

I don't hold with fancy patterns.

I've got to be honest and say that nowadays I very rarely elevate my decoys. It does take quite a lot of fuss and bother, and can be very time consuming, and in a high wind they're more than likely to fall out or look askew anyway. I also like to be able to move pretty quickly, and if I've got to mess about getting birds down from high trees, my freedom of movement is severely restricted.

What with your gun, cartridges, camouflage netting and decoys, you can see that there's quite a bit of gear to carry around with you. Sometimes, farmer willing, it is possible to drive your vehicle right up to the hide site and take the easy way out. Most of the time, though, it's up to you

to squelch around over the fields, up to your knees in mud, with half a hundredweight of gear on your back. I try to carry all my stuff in a couple of sacks, but I've seen people using bicycles with little carts behind and even golf trolleys. I have a friend who uses a really large backpack, which he bought from a mountaineering store. It is perfect. He can strap it on, walk about upright, have perfect balance and not be tired at all. It also means that his hands are free for opening gates or helping him climb over fences. Also, with a big backpack like this it doesn't really matter how muddy the ground is under the boot. He can walk through any sort of mire that would bog down carts in a second.

11 CONSTRUCTING A HIDE

When constructing a hide, you cannot afford to ignore the brilliance of pigeons' eyesight. I am quite convinced that they can easily see decoys a quarter of a mile away. If they can do that, just think from how far away they will be able to spot you and your gun glinting in the sunlight. That means that before you start building a hide you've got to consider your own appearance. It's not enough always to wear the same drab shooting clothes; sometimes you are going to have to look at the background, go to your wardrobe and select something new or a bit different that blends in more exactly.

Another preliminary consideration when setting up is that you have got to make sure that you are hidden all round. It's not as if pigeons just

A hide cunningly constructed behind a telegraph pole.

Can you see me? This is what I call a hide!

come in from in front of you where a good many people concentrate on being camouflaged. Pigeons come in from here, there and everywhere.

NATURAL HIDES

By far the best hides are natural ones. If you can get away without changing the landscape one jot, then that is the thing to do always. You've got to remember that pigeons build up a really exact picture of the ground beneath them, and anything new will stand out like a sore thumb. At the very best, they will treat it with caution.

I always look for a thick bush placed in the area where I want to shoot. One doesn't always happen to be growing conveniently, of course, but when it does, all you have to do is clear out a space in it and keep your head down. Look through the leaves and branches for birds coming in, and at the last moment stand up and let the

fun start. This isn't necessarily the most comfortable sort of hide, and you can have problems with vision all round you, but believe me, the pigeons will come over as though you weren't there at all. You can often shoot as many pigeons in an hour or so in a hide like this as you can in three hours when they're showing an element of cunning and caution.

The next best thing is to find a natural feature that will form part of a hide. I am thinking about ditches, hedges and trees especially. If you can build on a feature like this in the right position you are very lucky. All you're doing is taking a piece of the landscape and adding natural or well-camouflaged cover to it that will hide you as much as possible from the birds. Of all these features, the best is probably a ditch with a hedge behind it. Take everything into account that you can and then decide where you want to settle in the ditch and which way you expect to be looking out and firing. Then construct a hide around yourself

A natural hide.

A perfectly constructed hide.

using every bit of natural cover that will blend into the rest of the ditch and the hedge itself.

Take a lot of care with things that will soon die, especially if you can see yourself coming back to use the hide again in the future. Bracken looks good at first but soon withers and loses its colour and stands out badly. As soon as it turns pale, the game is given away. It can be the same with long grasses, so make sure that they fit in with the general colour of the hide and nothing looks out of place in any way. I even take a lot of care when I'm cutting branches or twigs back to trim the

view: these can look glaring white from up above, and I find that it pays to dampen the colour with a smear of mud or earth.

There will be times when it is important to have a roof, especially if the ground cover isn't too great, there isn't much wind, or there is a bright sun beating down. If you can, pitch your hide underneath the tree in a hedgerow, because that will break up your shape, even in mid-winter when the leaves are off. Failing a suitable tree, you might need to use a piece of netting, camouflaged with the usual hedgerow materials. Just

Camouflaged netting.

think carefully and make the thing as drab and inconspicuous as you can.

You cannot take any chances with camouflage. For example, when you get into the hide, make sure that any foliage is stroked back into position. If it lies wrong, it will catch the light and stand out as being unnatural, a real warning sign for every pigeon in the neighbourhood. If your hide is in an exposed position in the winter when the wind howls across open fields you might have to fasten everything together with wires, string or baler-twine and perhaps bang in a post or two to give the whole thing a bit of rigidity. This is important because if your hide begins to break up around you, then the pigeons will see it and be scared off – even if they don't see you sitting in there looking like a real idiot.

Do everything like this in plenty of time. A major hide like this takes a lot of time to secure and arrange, and you don't want to make a time-consuming mistake.

PORTABLE HIDES

If natural aids are really on the low side, you will have to import your own materials. I've found nets and poles provide the most useful portable hide, but remember that if you want an easy exit, you will need five poles, not just four. I've always found that the poles are made best by the local blacksmith. You'll need three of about five feet nine inches high and two just a bit longer at say six feet. The tops should be 'Y'-shaped to take the nets without a lot of extra tying. You need some sort of wedge or kicker near the bottom of each pole so that you can heel it hard into the ground. Army surplus camouflage netting is often used for hide making but the trouble with this is that it tends to be heavy, and plastic garden netting is gaining favour because it is much lighter and you can interlace it with straw or grass so that it is almost invisible and blends into the surroundings completely.

Hide camouflaged by branches, reeds and/or camouflaged netting.

Hide reinforced with garden fence wire or chicken mesh and held tight to hedge branches or tree for security

A reinforced hide.

I've got to be honest and say that I've never been entirely successful with a net hide out in the open, however carefully I've constructed it. I think you really do need some sort of background to break it up a bit. A simple post or a wire fence might do or even a water trough could provide some relief. I've even found that a clump of nettles will help or just a single, tiny bush – anything that will take the pigeon's eye off you.

There are those who like to build a hide out of old bales of straw. The main advantage of this kind of hide is the real comfort and luxury it pro-

vides. Bales give really good protection from the wind and the weather, and are perfect to sit on whilst waiting. You've also got room for equipment, and there aren't any overhanging branches and twigs to interfere with your range of fire. I usually make mine up as a square, each side consisting of bales stacked about three high. On three sides the bales are placed edge-up, and on the fourth – the one that faces the decoys I've put out – they are stacked side-up. This gives a lower side to shoot over with a higher background to disguise you and any movement you might make.

Wiring the hide together saves problems in a high wind.

A bale hide.

See how the hide merges into the hedgerow.

Apart from these bales, another can be used as a seat.

I'm afraid that I haven't had much luck with this kind of hide. I think one reason is that birds begin to associate bales with the bird scarers that are so common these days, and so they know to give them quite a wide birth. Also, you can never really hope to disguise a bale hide as anything remotely natural. It's always going to stand out like a castle in the field.

One last snag with bale hides is that they are cumbersome. Try moving thirteen often damp bales here and there. It will take you most of the morning I can tell you.

Whatever type of hide you settle on, make sure that you are as comfortable as possible. If you are sitting all squashed up and miserable, your patience is obviously going to wear out, and you're very likely to decide to move for home long before you should do. For a long session, a good firm seat is essential and a five-gallon oil drum has been a favourite with many experienced pigeon shooters for a long time. A friend of mine once gave me a shooting stick, but it tended to be too high and relatively unstable. You need to make your own decision and choose something that suits you, but remember that it is useful to have something

The pigeon shot at the ready!

that allows you to shoot from a sitting position if a bird comes in quickly and unexpectedly.

POSITION

So far I have put a lot of emphasis on the importance of not letting the birds see you, but don't forget that you have to see them. There is nothing more frustrating than having pigeons pass within range and being unable to shoot because of an obstruction – generally some branches that you have neglected to clear away. Do make sure that you have a pretty clear view of the sky.

This can be a problem with really thick hedge or even a bush, and you might have to do a bit of trimming out. However, always make sure that you ask a farmer's permission if you are going to do anything drastic. A lot of farmers won't be terribly keen to have pigeon shooters chopping their hedges around. It's all right perhaps if he knows and trusts you, and you are one of the few people shooting on his ground, but imagine what would happen if there was free access, and people took things into their own hands. Remember, you are always a guest on a farmer's field. Even if you are doing him a bit of good, you've got to behave responsibly. Otherwise, your name will soon get around the neighbourhood, I'll tell you.

Obviously the position of the hide is critical, and if you are in the wrong place then the best hide in the world will do no good whatsoever. I would therefore like to mention here just how useful binoculars are in helping you discover where the pigeons are and what they're doing. For static viewing, say from a car, 10 ¥ 50s are pretty good, but if you are carrying them around 7 ¥ 50s or 8 ¥ 40s are a lot better. I actually have a very small, light pair of 6 ¥ 30s, which are no problem to take to the hide with me. If I find that the shooting is relatively slow and I suspect I'm in the wrong place, at least I can look around me with the binoculars and form some impression of where I'd be better off. Just a hundred-yard move can make all the difference between a fairly poor day and a really good one.

I don't care what your gear is like, or your decoys, or even your shooting ability – over and over again I've come to realize that the person who gets the most pigeons is the one who really studies the territory and knows the flight lines of the birds and their favourite feeding grounds. Armed with this knowledge, he puts himself in exactly the right place at exactly the right time.

12 LAYING OUT DECOYS

There seems to be a great deal written in the press about decoy numbers and patterns these days. Sometimes I think that people just go around making things more complicated for the sake of writing an article and earning a bit of fame and some cash. In my view, it's not complicated theories that you need if you're going to bag good numbers of pigeons, but a profound knowledge of how the bird actually thinks and behaves.

NUMBER

In my view, and the view of the people who taught me, the more decoys that you spread on the ground, the better. It's as simple as that, but with just a few reservations. Look at it this way: the bigger the flock of decoys that you can put out the more likely live birds are to see them and come down with them. If you put twenty decoys out, you might think you've done well but there might be sixty real ones feeding just over the hill where you can't see them. Which group of pigeons do you think is most likely to attract others down from the air? As far as I'm concerned, it always pays to put out all the decoys you've got.

There are exceptions to this rule, however. One is when you are shooting over laid corn. By this I mean barley or wheat on long stems that has become top-heavy and then fallen prey to a good old blow or downpour. You will find that after a storm whole swathes of corn will lie flat in higgledy-piggledy patterns here and there around the field. Pigeons love this, and they will feed on even a green crop getting soft, milky pulp out of it, which they seem to love. Here, of course, if you put out too many decoys the real birds would not be able to find sufficient food and they might

fly off and look for a piece of ground that is not too crowded. The alternative is to look for a very large area of laid corn and really pile your decoys.

Another time when you can get away with using fewer decoys if you must is over a field of rape. Pigeons will feed on this in the very early stage when it is only two or three inches above the ground. The flock will really hit it then and because just a few decoys will be highly visible, you can get away without putting down great numbers. However, I've got to say that even in a situation like this, I would prefer to see twenty or thirty out there at least. To my mind, numbers attract numbers.

Linseed presents a similar situation to rape. Once the white shoots break through the ground, pigeons will go mad, and if there are no birds elsewhere on the field, this is another opportunity to work with just a few decoys. The field will look pretty barren and they will stand out well, so if you've only got a very limited amount of time to be out then it is well worth a try. This is much the case with any field that has been newly drilled: what decoys you put out will be highly visible and offer you the best chance of a shot or two without going to extreme lengths.

Obviously, if you're just taking up the sport and you can only afford ten or fifteen decoys, that is all you can put out to start with before moving on to freshly killed birds. I don't want to put you off shooting. The very purpose of this book is to encourage you and tell you what a marvellous sport it is. The fact remains, however, that as the years go by and you build up your numbers of decoys little by little, the number of pigeons you shoot is likely to increase as well.

I've been known to lay up to ninety decoys during a long session when pigeons were going

When the rain sheets down it shines on plastic decoys and gives the game away.

crazy on peas. Obviously, a lot of those were birds that I shot and set up afterwards on pointed sticks, but the whole effect was quite extraordinary. The birds simply gorged on the peas, and I could not have stopped them coming in even if I'd wanted to.

What I think happens is that the pigeons keep on the move, keep coming in, see a vast flock of decoys over a food they adore and just cannot resist coming down. I can remember on some occasions seeing more and more birds coming in even as I was reloading after a couple of success-

ful shots or after I'd just been out of the hide to set up some more decoys.

I have my own theories about why the sound of gunfire does not really bother pigeons any more. I'm sure it has to do with the craze for bird scarers that now dot our fields. These things go off 'Bang!' steadily throughout the day, and you notice that pigeon flocks barely even bother to raise their heads when they hear a shot. What was a good idea for a while has now been rumbled and is really next to useless. It only serves to annoy anybody in the vicinity trying to sleep in!

PATTERN

Some people advocate laying out decoys in complicated patterns to attract pigeons. More important, to my mind, than the actual pattern is where you set them in relation to your hide. You want to be shooting your birds at around twenty-five yards as a general rule of thumb. Once you move beyond thirty yards it gets very difficult indeed, and for that reason you do not want decoys so far away from you.

Placement depends a lot on the wind, and you have got to set the decoys out so that the wild pigeons coming in see them to best advantage.

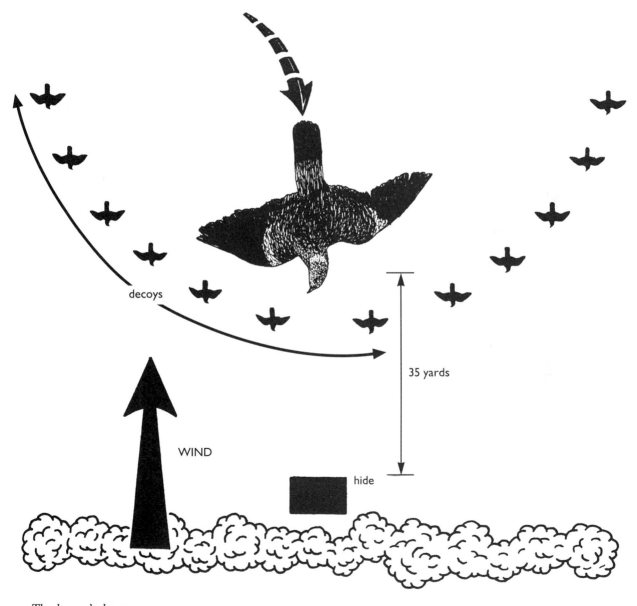

decoys

35 yards

WIND

hide

The decoyer's dream.

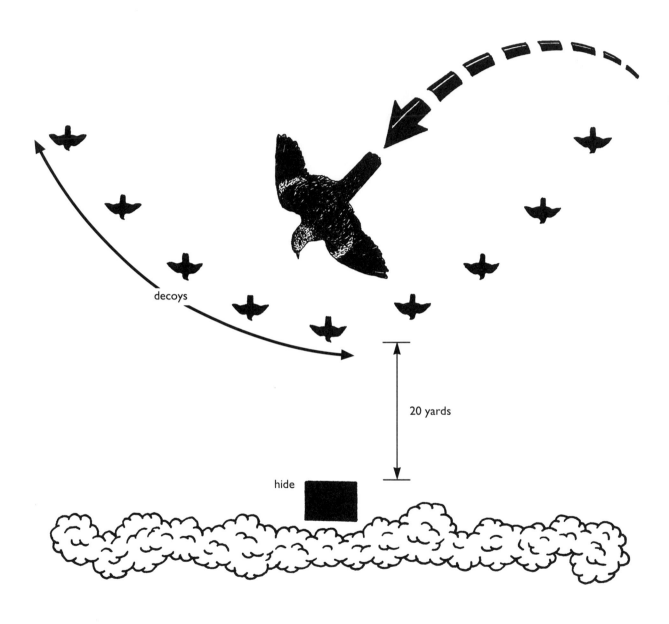

On a windless day, spread the decoy pattern.

There are no set shapes or patterns in the wild and you don't see any feeding pigeons set out neatly in the shape of a star or a horseshoe. I like to set up my decoys in a rough pattern over the area I want. If you lay the decoys out in too sym-metrical a fashion, they just won't look natural at all. Leave good spaces here and there and put a few others quite close together. That way things look natural, and you'll also find that the wild birds coming in have plenty of room to land and

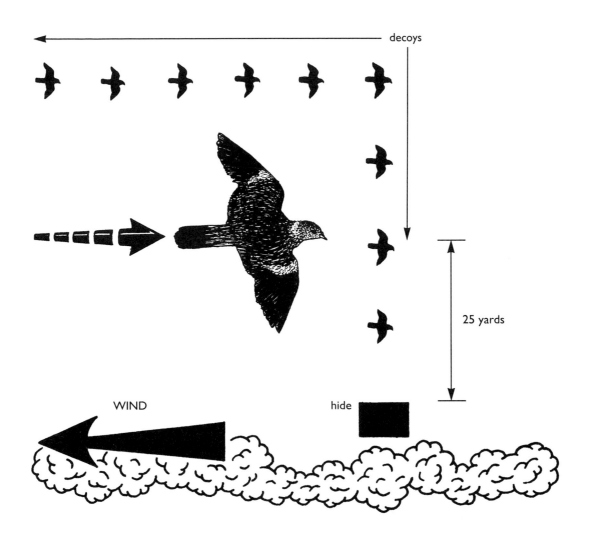

decoys

25 yards

WIND

hide

A change in decoy pattern brings the bird to the correct position for a shot.

start to feed – if you give them a chance that is!

When setting out decoys, the skill lies in making them look as natural as possible. Set a lot of them into the wind, but put a few here and there feeding from side to side, just as you see in a normal flock. Make sure that you do not let your decoys get blown over, as that will look unnatural. Everything has got to be done to make things look as realistic as possible.

I will sometimes put pigeons in a hedge, round the hide, just away from the main flock of decoys.

What you can do is fix them to a piece of wire that has a lead weight on the end. Put the pigeon and the wire over a branch and you will find that when the wind blows, the lead makes the pigeon move up and down just enough to look really quite natural. Half a dozen of these placed around the main pattern of decoys in front of you will do a very good job indeed. They are very easy to make and take only a minute or two to set up. There is no doubt that pigeons see these from quite a distance and will home in on the artificial flock.

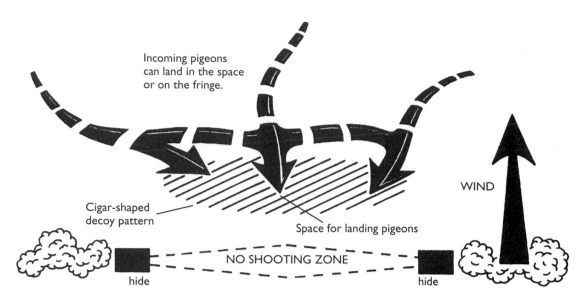

Incoming pigeons can land in the space or on the fringe.

Cigar-shaped decoy pattern

Space for landing pigeons

WIND

NO SHOOTING ZONE

hide

hide

The shared decoy.

Decoys being put up a 'sitty' tree by means of a lofting pole.

13 A REAL HOWLER

It was in the evening, and I had a call from Mike, the farm manager, telling me that pigeons were all over the field where he had been drilling the barley. He wanted to know if I could do anything about them. The poor man really did sound in a bad way and the least I could do was help him out and enjoy a bit of sport myself. I drove down early the next day to see what I thought, and he was right. The field was alive with pigeons coming out of the wood around, finishing off their breakfast. I watched them from a distance for a good while through binoculars and then got out of the vehicle and walked a fair bit of the hedgerow before deciding on a place to put up a hide.

The wind had been coming steadily from the south-west for a few days, and this was perfect for a hide on the end of a hedge that pushed well out into the field. I cut down a few thick branches of conifer and shoved them into the ground a good foot deep. (It was as well that I did in the end.) I also tied the whole thing together with string and rubbed mud on to the tops of the branches that

before

after

Mud-smeared branches.

I'd cut, to disguise the whiteness. Even the smallest things would turn the birds from the gun.

The killing ground was twenty to twenty-five yards in front of me, and I guessed the birds would come in from my right into the wind to settle in the area I would put my decoys. All seemed set to me, and I pulled off the farm road on to the lane overlooking the land. Through the binoculars I could see pigeons in the area, not at all concerned about the hide that I'd just put up. The situation just could not have been more promising.

That evening back at home I listened to the weather forecast, and it really was a horror: the wind would rise to gale or severe gale strength through the night, and it would bring heavy rain with it. Still, a night wind can often blow itself out by dawn, and I had high hopes. At first light, or just a little before, it seemed calm enough, but my cottage is surrounded by trees as befits a forester like me I suppose. Encouraged, I got up, put the kettle on, made my flask, roused the dog and we were soon away in the truck. That was when I realized my mistake. Out on the open road the wind simply howled, and the rain lashed down. It was like the end of the world with no light in the sky, but I was up and I decided to make the most of it.

I got the four-wheel-drive to the hide without cutting up the ride through the plantation at all. If I'd done that, Mike would not have thanked me. I unloaded two sacks of decoys, a bag with cartridges, a flask, a spare coat and a drum to sit on. Then I drove the truck back on to the hard road. The rain was still streaming down, and the ride would have got softer, so I didn't want to take any chances.

Keep low in the hide.

The wind was strong and it had changed direction a little since the day before – more west than south-west. This meant the pigeons would come in rather more from behind me than from the side. However, that couldn't be helped, and I would just have to do the best possible. I put the decoys out – thirty or so – not at all happy in the wind and the rain that kept trying to sleet and was driving constantly under my collar. Fortunately, I had a towelling cravat round my neck, which kept the drips from going down, and I was able to wipe my face with it every now and again when a blast really soaked me. Most of the decoys I put down facing the wind, but a few I placed here and there, like real birds moving out of the line to have a peck at something they'd seen.

Back in the hide I waited as I knew I'd have to for a bit of a lull in the weather. I was thankful for my one-piece waterproof suit and the fact that I'd made this hide as sturdy as I possibly could. The wind was gusting to sixty miles per hour but I didn't lose a single branch from the hide. Just imagine if I hadn't put it up strongly enough. There would be have been bits blowing around all over the fields, and soon I'd have been sitting there as bare as a plucked turkey.

At last I saw a clearer ridge of sky to the west and began to hope that the lull I needed was on the way. That was what the pigeons were waiting for too – I could actually see them through the binoculars in the lee of the wood across the meadow, huddled up against the weather, forsaking their breakfast in such foul weather. Still, delayed like this, there was every chance they'd be really hungry when the time came to get down to feeding.

Then up you get and follow the bird with the gun.

And down they come – both of them!

The rain and wind both eased as the clearer sky got closer. The rain actually died out completely for a while, and I knew then there would be some action. I was still worried about the wind though, now actually due west with even a bit of north to it at times! That meant the pigeons would be coming down the hedgerow behind me, and getting a shot in wouldn't be nearly as easy as I'd originally thought. Now I wasn't too happy about the hide, as I'd built it taller to the front and the side rather than towards the back. I hadn't expected the birds to be appearing round there. Nor was I really delighted with the decoys: the rain had made them glisten unnaturally, and the wind had blown one over on to its side. That would never do. I scampered out and righted it just before the first pigeons came over.

As I feared and expected, they were flying round the hedgerow behind me, fiercely into the wind, and I wasn't getting the clean shots that I'd

expected and set myself up for. They were also seeing me at the last moment as I stood up. To make things worse, I couldn't put on my balaclava like I normally do to mask the white – or should I say red – of my face. In all that sleet, it would have been sopping in a minute, and I'd have frozen my nose off. The wind was really whipping the birds away too, especially when they reached the edge of the hedge and got into its full force.

I got in just seven shots and hit four birds. Then, would you believe it, the sky clouded up, the sleet came back and the wind shifted even further north. I stuck things as best as I could for another fifteen minutes, but as there was no sign of a let-up at all, I decided to give it a rest.

I got out of the hide and grubbed up the decoys as quickly as I could. I hoisted the sacks over my shoulder and made off along the hedgerow. At least the wind was behind me now, and I was moving along like a ship under sail. The pigeons were back in the wood, laughing at me I suspect. The postman certainly did when I met him on the track. 'Mad bugger,' he said and gave me plenty of letters from that man we all hate called Bill! I got home to find that the fire was out, the room was dark and my wife was still in bed. Oh, and there was a tree down in the garden!

Even when I returned in the afternoon things didn't pick up a great deal. There were periods of sleet, and the wind was still fierce. Though there were pigeons about, they were only coming over in ones and twos. Then some walkers worked their way around the field, which quietened everything down a good deal I'll tell you. What on earth they were doing out on a day like that, the devil only knows. Finally, the sun came out, and I got a further five or six birds out of ten shots. It was a disappointing day in every way, especially considering how many pigeons were about the area.

I tell you about this experience just so you know that things don't always go according to plan. You've really got to face the weather and laugh at it if you can. I think it also proves that you might do everything as properly as you possibly can, and things will still conspire against you to ruin your day.

14 ROOST SHOOTING

Roost shooting is quite different from decoying in that you are getting the birds before they climb into bed rather than when they are up and about looking for their breakfast! Virtually all pigeon flocks will roost in woodland, hoping they are safe from predators in the trees and looking for shelter against the wind and frost. Certainly, winter is a good time to be out looking for roost shooting. If you can, get permission as soon as you can after 1 February, when the pheasant shooting finishes, but do take into account the wishes of the keepers.

At this time of the year they can be in the woods, catching up the hen pheasants, and obviously they won't want any disturbance. If you are asked by the keeper to wait until the end of February or the first or second week of March, don't be impatient, and don't try to break his rules. Remember always that the keeper is the best friend you could have, and it won't ever pay to cross him.

You will find that pigeons fly into the wind as they come into their roost. There is no such thing as a typical wood, but a diagram will give you some

The roost shooter well hidden by thick undergrowth.

70% of the pigeons roost in the back of the wood (sheltered from the wind).

30% of the pigeons roost in the middle of the wood.

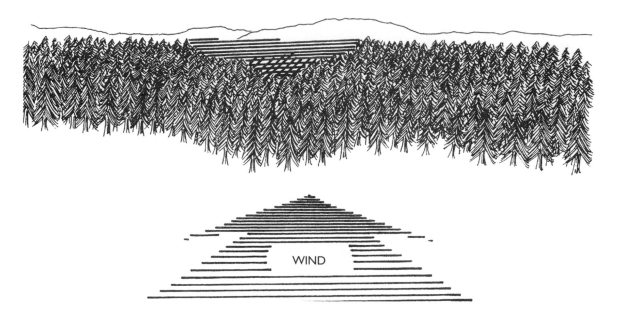

WIND

Pigeon roosting patterns.

idea. It is unlikely that there will be any pigeons settling in the fringe of woodland that faces the wind because it's just too cold for them. Even the next belt of wood tends to be avoided as decidedly chilly! You'll actually find that the majority will roost half-way into the wood, towards the back where it's more sheltered. They'll fly in and over with the wind then wheel off right or left and backtrack down into the canopy.

It can be hard to decide exactly when you want to get into the wood, and it always pays to be on the safe side. There's nothing worse than leaving things too late. Indeed, on some very bad days you'll find them in not long after lunch, especially when it's dark and cloudy and the days are very short. At times like this the whole flock could be in an hour or so before dusk, and if you're not early all you do is disturb them as you approach. Generally, it pays to get settled in around two hours before dark.

POSITION AND CAMOUFLAGE

Obviously, you have to think about your position in the wood. If there is a lot of rubbish at the base of the trees, you might not need a hide in the real sense. You can probably root about and make a hollow in the fallen branches where you'll be well hidden. Even though the light will be fading it's important to wear camouflage clothing. Think about this carefully because you need to match the colour and tone of the woods. An ordinary camouflage jacket can be too pale for a conifer wood and then again too dark for the pale grey of ash woods. You might find that a dark wax jacket or any old clothing of dark greens and browns is better for the conifers. If you are in an ash wood, you may prefer some pale tweed, which will merge in with the trees perfectly.

But what about up above? Where exactly are the birds going to land? Pigeons love tall trees to land

A perfect surveying sight for a pigeon or two.

in, and they will probably go in at a high level and settle for a time while they spy out the land. They could be looking for predators on the outskirts of the wood or for any dangers within. They could also be looking for their bed in the canopy when the time comes. I think mainly they are resting. Any tall tree on the fringe of the wood will be a favourite for this, especially if it towers some twenty to forty feet above the main woodland. You'll find that plenty of pigeons will come in, make for this spot and act as living decoys. Therefore, it's best not to shoot at the first one or two birds.

If you are wondering where to stand in the wood itself, remember that clumps of evergreen trees or heavily ivy-clad trees are a good draw in a deciduous wood, and the pigeons will go there for that little bit of extra shelter. Larch trees, if

Pigeon droppings in the wood give you a good clue to their roosting whereabouts.

they are present in the wood, often seem to attract birds as well. The most mature trees in the wood are the ones that are most stable and sway the least in heavy winds. Pigeons seem to like these secure bedposts, so look out for a position close to such a tree if you can find one.

It's a good idea to stand against a good-sized bush or a big tree trunk. Remember that you need to be able to see the birds quite well, but you also want to be hidden as much as possible. Something that can disguise your shape is invaluable. I'm not sure about hats. A lot of people recommend flat hats with brims that shield the white of your face. Obviously it's important to keep that flash of white down to a minimum, especially when dusk is coming and the wood is getting dark. However, I've always found that a hat can restrict your vision.

I'm a great believer in getting things sorted out early on and not leaving anything to the last moment. I always like to assess a wood a little bit beforehand, if possible before the day I'm actually shooting. You should get around into as many woods as you possibly can and see which the pigeons are using at the time. If you keep your eyes open, you'll probably be able to judge by the droppings which trees are favourites! Pigeons have splashy, white droppings that are really quite visible and stand out well. The more you learn about the wood, the more confident you'll feel in what you're doing, and that's very important.

Choose your tree cover carefully. It's very tempting to look for a gap in the canopy where you've got a good sighting of birds coming over. The trouble is, of course, if you can see them, you can bet your hide that they can see you even better, and they'll tend to veer away at that vital moment when your finger is on the trigger. For some reason, pigeons find it much more difficult to spot you if they've got to look through a few branches. Of course, if the branches are too thick, then you will have problems seeing them or even getting a shot through. Perhaps the best bet is to look out for an area where the tree cover above is patchy and spread out a little, so that you will get a view, but your shape will be broken up by plenty of foliage.

The dog, the birds and the hide! Pigeon shooting in a frame.

In the end you will find that it is up to the individual. Experience will lead you instinctively to the right spots. The best thing is to assess the situation for yourself, on-site, and preferably in good light before the birds start coming in. Don't put your-

self under pressure, or you'll get panicky, soon lose trust in your spot and begin to want to move.

There isn't necessarily anything wrong with moving, however, if you've got the time. If you know that the birds are coming in and you are not getting enough shots, it makes sense to have a move to see if things pick up. All the time you should be thinking where you can position yourself to do the best job, and providing you keep thinking and experimenting, success won't be that far away.

WEATHER CONDITIONS

Weather conditions are very important. It can get desperately cold in the late afternoon even in the heart of a wood, so it makes sense to choose the best weather you can. Wind can chill to the bone if it carries rain and sleet. You are not shooting to live, only for sport and to help out a farmer, so there is no point going out on such a day unless really dressed for it. Ideal conditions are windy and dry.

The quieter the sky is, the higher the pigeons will come in, and they'll only drop down on their last approach to the wood, giving you next to no chance at all. Another problem is that when the weather is calm, flock sizes tend to be larger. Sometimes all you get is a sighting of one big group of birds coming in high and fast because the next second they're behind you, safe in the wood, tucked up for the night. There's nothing more exasperating, I can tell you. On the other hand, providing a mild, often westerly wind continues to blow, you'll find that the flocks break up, and pigeons will come in – in twos or threes – over a much longer period, giving you the chance to get in plenty of shots through the late afternoon.

I've always enjoyed shooting in the snow. Snow clouds keep warmth in, and if there's a bit of wind too then things will work nicely to your advantage. If there is a lot of snow on the ground, I sometimes wear a sheet that I belt around me so that it does not flap in the breeze and give the game away. However, this isn't always necessary.

I also love to be out on misty, foggy nights. I suppose this is the one time when wind is not that important because pigeons come over both low and slow, and of course you're better hidden than ever in the soupy air. The combination can sometimes be lethal. I suppose the drawback is that you get less time to see the pigeons come, but the advantages always outweigh the disadvantages.

SHOOTING STYLE

It's amazing how many people miss bird after bird when they are roost shooting. I've seen some blokes so exasperated they threaten to sell their guns the very next day, but if you obey a few rules, then things will certainly look up. For example, it really does pay to try to get into the habit of putting the gun into your shoulder right at the last moment. That way the pigeons see the movement only late on, hopefully when it's too late to do much about it. If you need to, practise the movement by yourself over and over. Remember it's mount, swing and pull the trigger, in one fluid movement.

First shot of the night!

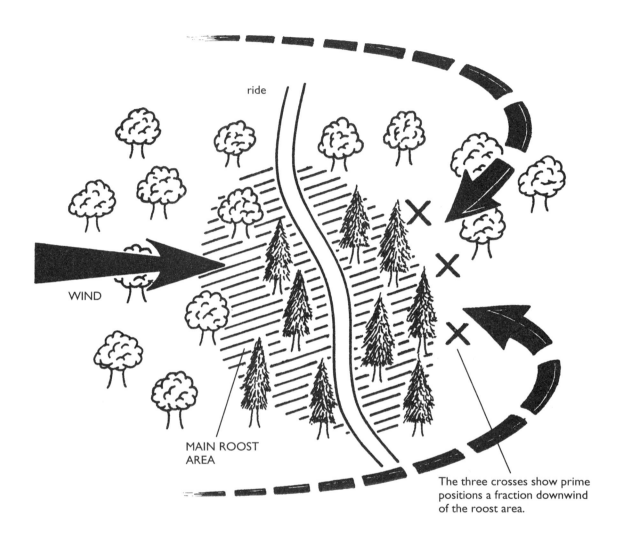

ride

WIND

MAIN ROOST
AREA

The three crosses show prime
positions a fraction downwind
of the roost area.

A typical night roost.

Another rule is to wait till the very last moment when the pigeon is at its lowest before you shoot. All too often guns get wildly excited and pop off at any bird they see, even those far too high to be hit with any degree of success. I always wait till I can see the whites of their eyes, so to speak, even through the dusk! If you try shooting at imposs-ible targets, all you'll do is scare other birds that were probably coming in lower behind them. Remember that you are probably not the only person in the woods. If you keep insisting on tak-ing higher shots, you will scare the birds off for everybody else, and you'll get some black looks when you assemble back on the ride.

Strangers in the wood can be a bit of a problem unless you meet up beforehand and work out some sort of strategy. It is much better to get some friends together and decide to shoot a wood one evening. If you have a gun in two or three woods over a tight area, you'll find that the shooting tends to break the birds up, keeping them on the move and prolonging the sport for everybody.

15 TOWERS

Probably the most exciting form of roost shooting that I know is shooting from a tower that you've built in woodland. You are right up there, in the clouds almost, with the birds as they are coming in to roost. It's hard to forget the feeling of excitement as the birds begin to come, zinging around your very head, so close that you feel you could almost touch them sometimes. If you put the tower in the right place, this can be one of the most productive forms of pigeon shooting there is.

Above all you've got to choose a wood with care. Building a tower takes a lot of work and expense, so you need to know that the wood is yours for a good while. You need to have assurances that it will be possible to leave the tower there, add to it and use it for many years to come.

My big weakness is smoking – see how that puff of smoke is a real giveaway.

Tower hide in amongst conifers.

The last thing you want is to go to a great deal of effort putting up a tower only to lose access to the wood in a year or so. I would never consider putting a tower up in a wood where I wasn't absolutely sure of my future.

Providing you've got all the permissions, the next step is to decide exactly where in the wood to put your tower. My advice is to site it in one of the most thickly treed areas. In the first place it will blend in well there. This is important for the birds and the landowner. The less obvious the tower is, the happier both pigeons and owners will be. Don't forget that camouflage is always important when it comes to pigeon shooting, especially when you are up in the canopy. If there aren't enough tree tops around, then you will stand out like a sore thumb, and the pigeons will soon learn to avoid your tower.

In the second place, there is a much greater chance of trees going over in a gale in areas where the wood has been thinned out. Where the trees are few and far between, they have little protection from the wind. In fact, it's worth checking with the owner of the wood that he'll leave the area around the tower alone and not want to clear it. Most owners are amenable to this, and quite a few of them even like to use the towers themselves for various reasons.

There's no point at all in skimping on materials when it comes to building a tower. Always use the best. If you don't, you'll find that things begin to go wrong with it after a couple of years, and soon it will be worse than useless, even dangerous. Think how bad you would feel if the wood owner's son got up there and took a tumble. Find the strongest steel that you can buy; make sure that you concrete the legs into the earth. I can't over state how important it is to have a firm base for your tower. The footings have to support your weight and the weight of the structure, and hold everything firm in even the strongest wind. If you just put the legs into soil, you will find that they can easily work loose after a while, especially if the ground is sandy or peaty.

Always make sure that you have a good-sized base and that you work up in a very gentle pyramid, though of course it will never be sharp at the top! Rather, you need a sturdy, safe platform up there to work from. You don't want something flimsy or uncomfortable. All your attention needs to be focused on the pigeons, and you don't want to be worried about what is going on beneath you.

Remember to build in the facility to add a storey to your tower every two or three years as the trees about you grow. The wood won't stand still just because you've built a tower in it, and if you haven't thought this out, the trees will leave you behind, and your tower will be next to useless.

Ideally, the platform will be about five feet from the tops of the trees so that when you stand up you are just above the branches and have a good clear view without being too obvious to the pigeons as they come in to land. This is critical, because if you are too low you won't get a clear shot. Too high and you will give the game away. Get it just right, and you will find that you will see the pigeons without being too obvious to them.

It is vital to have room at the top of the tower so that you can move about a bit and change angle according to the wind and the way the pigeons are flighting. Make sure that the safety-rail is a really strong one and that it goes all the way round the platform at the top. The last thing you want is to fall at dusk, especially holding a gun. Equally, you need a good firm ladder up the tower. Don't be tempted to take any short cuts when it comes to this.

If you put a tower up, do think carefully about how many times you will shoot that wood. Tower shooting is probably one of the most exciting ways of killing a pigeon there is, but you must not overdo it, or they will soon learn to avoid the wood and shooting will go down a great deal. As a result of this, I tend to shoot only once a month from a tower, no matter how big the temptation is to get up there every few nights. In the same way, it doesn't make a lot of sense to shoot over decoys in the fields around the tower, because you'll only alert the birds in the area, and you may find that they soon begin to move off. Act sensibly, not greedily, and you'll find that the tower serves you very well over many years.

Ideally, I like the late afternoon, which has a good wind about it – one that comes from

A well-camouflaged hide – perfect for roost shooting.

Part of a big bag of pigeons.

the west or south perhaps, so that it is not too cold. Remember that up there you really are out with the gods and if the wind is biting or if there is sleet about you really feel it. If you choose a breezy but mild day, you will enjoy the whole experience, and your shooting is bound to be that much better.

Having a tower not only affords you a terrifically successful and exciting way of shooting pigeons as they come in to roost, it has other bonuses. One of the interesting things about all animals is that they hardly ever look up. They seem to be too busy looking at the floor for any

food or sniffing the air at nostril height. They don't really think of danger coming from up above, so if you are in the tower, you stand a good chance of seeing badgers, foxes and deer coming very close to you indeed. For that reason alone, a lot of wood owners are happy for you to build a tower because it means that they can use it when you are not shooting and reap a massive amount of enjoyment from their property. It's nice when pigeon shooters and country lovers can work together in this fashion. Co-operation like this can only be a good thing in the countryside, and it's good when we all pull together.

16 JAMES' WOOD

I really love pigeon shooting in James' Wood for all sorts of reasons, especially when the wind comes in from the north. It's a really big old conifer wood that attracts a great many birds. I think that's partly because it's not frequently shot, being in the middle of a large private Estate, and the birds have a good deal of confidence

A dead tree like this one hit by lightning will often be attractive to a pigeon as it decides on its night roost.

here. Also, it's quite a distance from the nearest house – a cottage with a very quiet old couple in it that's half a mile away at least. Of course I don't cook my own goose – if that's the right expression! I could have excellent shooting in the fields around it, but I don't think one can really have cake and eat it when it comes to pigeon shooting. If I did that, the pigeons would become wary of the entire area, and while they might still use the wood, it certainly wouldn't be in the numbers or with the confidence that they do at the moment. If you've got something really good, it doesn't pay to spoil it.

There are other things, too, that make the wood what it is: for instance, the lie of the land. The meadow to the north is steep at the brow but dips sharply as it reaches the trees. This allows the pigeons to swoop down low, looking for the shelter the tree belt gives them. Of course, when they come down low, I'm there waiting for them!

I've got a couple of extra favourite spots just inside the fence of the wood, and there is one in particular that's often the best. The tree-line is broken just that little bit, giving me a good few gaps through which to take careful shots. However, there are quite enough branches around to cover up my face. You needn't bother about shooting through branches, providing that they're not too thick. You do need a decent view of the birds to get a shot in, especially when the light begins to go, and they're coming in fast.

There are lots of dead old branches and debris on the floor here, all in a dip too. There's hardly any need for me to build a hide. I can get deep down in there and stand at the last minute. If I'm in the sort of mood to want to stand all the time, there are one or two big old tree trunks just around the dip that I can lean against so that my

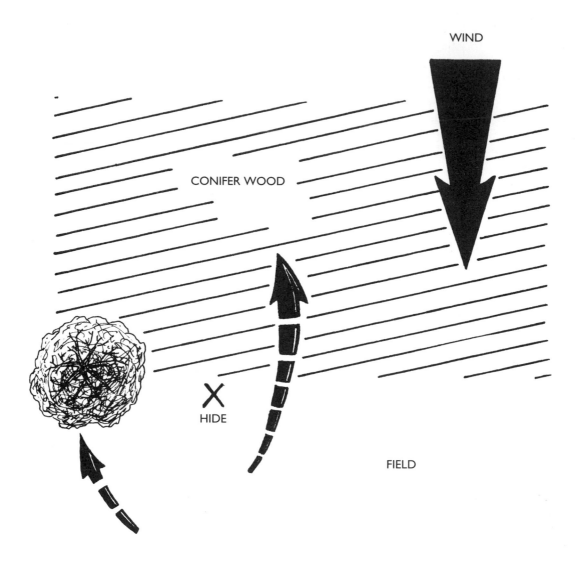

WIND

CONIFER WOOD

X
HIDE

FIELD

Pigeons flock to roost in the wood, sometimes via the big oak tree.

outline is well camouflaged. I suppose the fact that I go back to this spot every now and again through the winter makes it a favourite for me. My confidence in it rises, and therefore I concentrate harder, put in more time. Of course, I don't overshoot the wood by any means. I drift in every few weeks to see what's about. That way, the birds never really get too worried and continue to use the wood as a major roosting site.

There is a big oak tree at James' Wood, about sixty feet tall. The top ten-foot section is quite dead, and almost every night pigeons come in to settle there for a few minutes, getting their breath, surveying the scene. Only then will they go into the wood. I'll leave the first few that land there, as they attract more in, and that way I get my own roosting decoy. If things are very slow, I can take a pot at them, which gets me a bird or

A perfect pigeon wood-roosting site the year through.

A typical 'sitty' tree.

two and stirs up the whole wood. I don't really like shooting at sitting birds but sometimes it's just got to be done. An old trick is to aim at the feet of the bird, and it does seem to work. However, it does always appear that I miss many more than I hit when it comes to sitters.

There's always something to watch in this wood, and that's another thing I like about it. You can see where deer have taken the bark off the trees here and there, and there are at least two badger setts. Here and there the animals have been digging up the bluebell bulbs – they're all scattered about, and the peaty soil lies everywhere. Just along the way there's the remains of a tree that came down in a gale years back. The badgers have used that as a scratching post for as long as I can remember. It's wonderful to be able to get so close to nature.

17 DOGS AND THE PIGEON SHOOTER

Well done, boy!

First let me say that dogs, to my mind, are no use at all when shooting over decoys. Of course, there are those who disagree and take their dogs with them all the time, but if you let a dog out of the hide to go to retrieve the shot pigeons, any fresh birds coming in will immediately take alarm. After all, what pigeons would sit there immobile and apparently uncaring while a gun dog runs amok amongst them? I suppose it can be done if

you let the dog out and whistle him back pretty promptly, but even so I don't think there's a great deal of need, providing you keep your eyes on the birds as they are falling and make sure you retrieve them all when it's time to go or at intervals throughout the shooting.

I would also say at this point that you must not take a dog on to somebody else's land unless you have permission. By and large, keepers are wary

A dog certainly has his uses!

of having a dog running about, especially off a lead, and they will be furious if they see a dog loose at laying time especially. There's not a great deal of point taking a working dog anywhere on a lead for long periods of time. You're not doing the dog or yourself any particular favours. A working dog is meant to work!

There are, however, occasions when a dog can actually be of some use. I suppose having a dog with you is most handy when it comes to roost shooting, because it can be really quite useful to send a dog out to pick up birds as the light is fading. It's good for the dog, and it's good for you.

However, you have to be in total control of your dog. He's got to obey your instructions down to the last letter if he's going to be of any help.

I've got a working golden Labrador, and as you can guess he has a problem when it comes to camouflage. He simply stands out like a sore thumb, and pigeons see him miles away, even if I'm well hidden up behind a tree trunk. Thus, I've got to make sure that he stays in a hide or under some brambles so that the pigeons don't see him. Fortunately, he is well trained, and he will stay totally still wherever he's instructed. If he weren't like that, then I could never take him with me.

A dog can also be useful when you're roughing-up. By that I mean going out, possibly in the afternoon of a dull day, when there's a fair bit of wind, to see what there is about. Rabbits are probably top of the list, but you'll find that pigeons are about too, and you might well get in a shot or so. At times like this a dog will prove a really useful companion, retrieving anything that you might bring down.

I also like to take my dog with me when I'm simply walking an area, spying out the land for pigeon shooting to come. It's nice to have the dog with me and to give him some exercise: it's all too easy for a working dog to get out of trim and begin to put on weight. I like to give him lots of exercise, especially in the early autumn before pheasant shooting begins in earnest, when he really does work for his keep.

CHOOSING A DOG

The choice of a dog is rather up to you. As well as my Labrador, I've got a terrier. I find her useful for rats and so on, but I tend not to take her out pigeon shooting lest she disappears off down a badger sett and comes up with no head. Terriers are fine little dogs, but you've got to be careful of them in certain areas of countryside. I've also had spaniels in the past, and I love them as well. I've always found spaniels very hard-working dogs, and an advantage that they have over Labradors is that they really love brambles. Ground can't be rough enough for a spaniel. You'll find that a Labrador will go round a heap of brambles, but a spaniel will just leap in with its tail wagging.

Whichever breed you choose, you've still got to buy the right dog, and a lot of that comes down to

The well-trained gun dog …

... brings the bird willingly to hand.

what you can afford. These days you can easily pay up to £500 for a really good Labrador puppy of a high pedigree. However, I've got to say that I've seen many high-pedigree dogs that haven't worked nearly as well as run of the mill keepers' dogs. That's where I got my dog: he came of one keeper's bitch and another keeper's dog. I can't remember the exact figure, but I think he cost me something between £80 and £100. (There may have been a bit of wood or something else thrown in to round figures up a bit.)

What I like about my dog and dogs like him is that they come from really good working stock.

His ancestors were gun dogs and working dogs, and somehow this type of life is bred into the genes. There's really something there for you to work with.

TRAINING

Of course, there's a great deal in training dogs, and there is a lot said about training dogs in the countryside with which I don't really agree. Many, for example, say that you've got to starve your dog to train him, but I've never done that or found it even remotely necessary. I simply praise my dog when he's good, and I'm harsh – with my voice that is – when he deserves a good ticking off. I've never hit a dog yet, and I don't intend to. Swearing at him is another thing altogether, and I'll give him a good old yell if he deserves it.

I suppose I've learnt a great deal about training dogs from watching keepers with their animals. A keeper's dog has to be like a brother to him, really dedicated to the job. All the best keepers' dogs I've known have responded simply to the tone of the voice without any need to resort to cruelty or harshness whatsoever.

I don't know why, but it's always seemed to me that you can train a bitch that little earlier than a dog, but whatever you do, don't try and rush the animal and overdo things at the start. For the first three or four months you've simply got to play with the animal and make him feel at home with you. You need to build up a trust between you, but you've also got to make sure that you're the boss.

Get him to stay, sit and so on, and reward him with a little titbit whenever you think he's done well.

Proper training can begin after four or five months, and you can take it from there, stretching the dog to an extent but not setting out to confuse him in any way. It's never a bad idea to train a young dog with an older one, providing the old one sets a good example and puts the puppy right whenever he steps off the right track.

You can have great fun training a dog, and both of you will enjoy it. Your dog will always enjoy your company and going out working for you if you treat him properly from the start. Believe me, whenever you pick up a gun, he'll cock his head.

Never take him for granted and don't run him into the ground. In peak condition, you can work a dog about three times a week, but do be careful and watch his condition carefully because dogs can easily become very tired. At best, a dog will be a constant friend, companion and a real help.

18 THE HELPING HAND

If, as pigeon shooters, we regard ourselves primarily as sportsmen who are helping out the farmer by ridding his fields of a major pest, then there are other vermin we should bear in mind. You will find that the more you help the farmer out with his various trials and tribulations then the more likely he is to accommodate you in the winter when he wants pigeons culled.

Never underestimate how great the need is to clear out some vermin. Although many of us like to see foxes on the land, we've got to realize that they breed almost without check and could throw the whole of nature out of balance if we're not careful. Many people lament the killing of a few foxes, yet they love to see hares and partridges. You can't have too many foxes if you're going to have those! As far as farmers are concerned, foxes are deadly when it comes to poultry and will even take lambs in the early part of the season. They will wreak havoc in a pheasant wood.

Keeping down the farm vermin.

The weasel is a great predator on pigeon nests close to the ground.

Rabbits are almost as big a problem as pigeons, especially when the soil is sandy. This encourages them to burrow into the soft land and make their home there to breed. Rabbits can be a real plague. I know one farmer who believes that he has something like a few thousand rabbits on his land – that's at least ten to twelve to each acre – and they do a great deal of damage to his peas, his corn, his sugarbeet and virtually everything else that you can name. In fact, he is reduced to driving around each evening with his dogs and gun, just shooting what he can get. He has his gamekeeper after them all the time, but still he is overrun. You can guess how welcome I am over there to give him a bit of a helping hand from time to time.

Then there is the grey squirrel, which in many people's eyes is nothing more than a tree-rat. The problem with the greys as far as the naturalist is concerned is that they have been largely responsible for ousting the red squirrel from most parts of Britain. Where the red is being re-introduced, precautions have been taken against the grey. It seems that it is not a question of the two species competing for food. Rather, the problem comes during the mating season. A red squirrel weighs considerably less than a grey, and it is not uncommon to see a single red female pursued by a horde of large grey males with just one thing on their minds! You can imagine what happens to the poor red when she's caught. Recently, I have been charged with clearing a wood of greys, simply to see if we can re-introduce some reds, and believe me it has not been easy. As soon as I turn my back, some more greys creep in from somewhere.

As far as farmers are concerned, the grey squirrel is a real pest when it comes to wheat and barley, especially as they get ripe. Greys are also terrors for nibbling the new shoots out of conifer woods, and they do a great deal of damage to hard wood, especially to the beech and sycamore when they nibble off the bark and let the sap show. In short, the grey squirrel is a pest.

I should also mention rats. They can be a menace around the farmyard and seem to get into everything that is stored. Then there are stoats and weasels too that wreak havoc with poultry and pheasants. I suppose I could continue about moles that turf up the pasture and even magpies and jays that take chicks from the poultry yard by the dozen.

However, I don't want to give the impression that the pigeon shooter should run amok in the countryside. On the contrary, he should always respect the farmer's wishes. For example, hares do a fair bit of harm but virtually everybody likes to see these graceful creatures, and it's very unlikely that you will be encouraged to do anything about them – nor should you want to, in my view.

What sort of equipment do you need if you are going to perform these other little tasks for farmers? For rabbits and squirrels the shotgun that you use for pigeons will be absolutely perfect. You could use a rifle, but remember that the land has to be surveyed by the local police before you shoot through it.

Things are a little bit different for foxes, and I would certainly advise going after them with a high-powered rifle that needs a firearms certificate from the local constabulary. A .225 is a big rifle and is made specially for sport like fox shooting. The ammunition needs to be very high velocity. It will have a soft point to do the damage inside the animal. The last thing that you want is to cause any lasting pain and suffering, and that's why I would not recommend the use of a shotgun for clearing foxes – unless you are sure of a close-range shot. Never take any chances with a loose shot that might just maim an animal.

As this is a book about pigeon shooting, I won't go into tremendous detail with lots of hints about clearing up other vermin, but I would like to give a few pointers. If you are out after a fox or two, remember that summer is not really the time because it is a period of great growth, in the field, in the woods and in the hedgerows. Your only chance of shooting a fox in the summer is if you know its movements, and you can catch it out in the open, which takes some doing, I can tell you.

The best time to go out after foxes is after the harvest, on the stubble at night. You'll find foxes there in plenty, both hunting and travelling. The thing to do is to range a lamp over the ground until you pick up the eyes of a moving animal. Then, squeak the fox in. By that I mean that you should make tiny squeaking noises that sound like a small rabbit or other animal in distress. That will naturally arouse the hunting instincts of the fox, and unless he has been shot at before, he'll come in and investigate. In fact, I've often picked up a fox in the lamp at about three or four hundred yards and squeaked him in till he's come to within thirty paces or so. The big thing is that you must be downwind of the animal (exactly the opposite of where you want to be with pigeons), otherwise, the fox will scent you at once and clear off very quickly indeed. The other thing is to make sure that your body is not silhouetted against any light background or again he will take fright.

It is traditional to use a red lamp when foxing, and I suppose that stands less chance of frightening the fox off than a white one, but I would stress that a red lamp should only be used with extreme caution where you are absolutely sure of your ground. Let me give you the example of a very near miss that a friend of mine experienced when using a red lamp.

He knew the ground in front of him should be free of people and that nobody should be on the Estate at all. Soon enough, he picked up a pair of eyes at about two hundred and fifty yards range. Those eyes didn't move at all, and though he squeaked and squeaked they did not approach. Looking through his powerful telescopic sights, he could not make out what the eyes belonged to, which made him just a little bit suspicious. The

Freedom means walking with the gun in pigeon country – the gun always open.

more suspicious he became, the more he decided not to shoot. In the end he decided to put on a white light and see what was going on. There, sitting by a pond, without any permission at all, was an angler with his pet Alsatian dog. If my friend hadn't been an experienced and sensible person, he might have seen those eyes and let go with a bullet.

I would say that you have to be really experienced in the ways of foxes before you start using a red light, because you don't want any risk whatsoever of taking out a dog, a deer or even a human. You must leave anything alone that you're not sure about. At least a white light gives you far better vision and lets you see exactly what's out there.

Things are a lot less complicated with rabbits and squirrels because after all you're shooting them pretty much in the daylight. My favourite time for rabbits is early morning, especially when there's mist about and it's been a pleasant night. Then you'll find them out on the crops, getting their last food before siesta. Equally, the evening is good because then they're coming in to feed after the heat of the day. Remember that rabbits have a tremendous sense of smell, so you've got to approach them with the wind in your face if you're going to stand any chance.

You can walk round the woods looking for squirrels with your normal pigeon shotgun and do very well. Look out for the drays, the places where they live and nest. The big tip here is to use a large stick and tap the bottom of the tree that holds a dray. You might have to tap quite hard a good few times, but sooner or later out will come the squirrel and sit on the branch looking at you. If the tree is small, you can achieve the same effect by rocking it. You can often find out where these drays are by looking for slivers and slices of pine cones. Squirrels take these back to their drays where they eat them and throw down the unwanted bits, advertising their presence.

Let me say before finishing this chapter that you should only do these sort of things to help out the farmer and clear the land of a few pests, so that crops and other animals in need of a bit of protection can flourish. Everything in nature needs to be balanced. The pigeon shooter can perform quite a valuable role if he is sensible and doesn't overdo things.

19 PIGEON FOR THE POT

It seems to me that pigeons fit very well with the sort of thinking I hear today about food. You see, you could not get a purer, less polluted meat than pigeon. I suppose they do eat crops that have been chemically dressed, but a great deal of their food is taken from wild plants and clover, which are absolutely free of any artificiality.

I've got to tell you that I'm not much of a cook myself, but I have picked up a fair bit just from watching and occasionally even doing! First let me say that pigeons are about the easiest birds to pluck that you'll find. The feathers almost float off the body. In fact, they carry on floating and end up absolutely everywhere! If you've got any sense at all you'll pluck your pigeon out of doors where the feathers won't be too much of a problem. With bigger birds, I tend to put a piece of string over a branch and tie it to the bird's legs. That way both hands are free to pluck.

It has to be said, however, that virtually all the meat from a pigeon is on the breast, and for many recipes all you need to do is peel back the unplucked skin from the breasts and take these out with a sharp knife. This might sound extravagant, but I guess ninety per cent of the meat is there, and if you've got a lot of pigeons you won't find the time for a really big plucking session.

Remember that the pigeon's liver contains no gall, so you are safe to leave it inside the bird when you are cooking. It even gives a bit of extra flavour. You couldn't dream of doing this with a pheasant, for example, because if it got ruptured the whole taste of the bird would be tainted.

Remember that there is no close-season for pigeons, and I feel that they are at their best – that is plumpest – when they have been living off the cream of the farmers' crops between May and October. Another point to bear in mind is that a young pigeon has softer, pinker legs than an old one and a round plump breast. In fact, to my mind there's nothing to beat a good, fresh squab (a small pigeon five or six weeks old). You will find the meat more tender. Finally, you don't need to hang pigeons, as you do pheasants for example, but I always make a point of cleaning their crops out as soon as possible.

RECIPES

Probably the best way to cook squabs, or at least plump pigeons, is to roast them. You clean the pigeons well and put some parsley or mixed herbs with some softened butter, salt and pepper into each bird. You truss the birds up, cover with slices of streaky bacon and then place them in a hot oven (200°C, 400°F, Gas mark 6) for just over twenty minutes. It's good to have some butter left over with which you can baste the birds every few minutes. Just before serving, remove the fatty bacon and sprinkle on a little flour so that the breasts brown up nicely. Allow one bird per person.

If the pigeons are slightly older, then it's better to casserole them. I like this done in either cider or beer. You simply place the pigeons close together in a casserole with a covering of sliced onions. Then pour over the cider or the beer (a stout is quite nice) and add some garni, mace and stock. You put them in quite a slow oven (170°C, 325°F, Gas mark 3) for about two hours. It pays to try them a few times, because they may become tender before then. Remove all the garni and thicken the gravy, which you pour over the birds when you serve.

Probably my favourite recipe of all is pigeon breast pie. You simply cut out the breasts with a sharp knife (allow three breasts per person). For every three breasts, add one hard boiled egg and a couple of ounces of bacon cut into strips. Simmer the breasts first of all in half a pint of stock or water with a little pepper and salt in it. Then remove all the meat from the bones and put it into a pie dish with alternate layers of bacon and

Carrying a few birds to the freezer for use as future decoys.

a sliced hard boiled egg. If you want, you can add some of the liquid that the breasts simmered in and season with salt. Then cover with flaky pastry and bake in a hot oven until the pastry is cooked. Then cook at a lower heat for thirty or forty minutes to make sure the bacon is ready as well. It should be served hot, but you can take it out cold with you the next day, and it is still delicious. A few mushrooms can add a little flavour to the pie for a change now and again.

Pigeon breasts are also very nice with cabbage. Cut the cabbage into very fine slices making sure that all the hard bit is removed. Then par-boil the cabbage in salted water for seven minutes before draining all the water away. Wrap each pigeon breast in a slice of streaky bacon and secure it with a tooth-pick. Then brown the breasts in bacon fat and lay them on a layer of cabbage that has been put in a deep casserole dish. Then add onion, carrots and even juniper berries if you can find them along with salt and pepper and nutmeg. Cover up the whole lot with some more cabbage and put in a stock. This should then be covered with grease-proof paper and a tight-fitting lid. Cook in a cool oven for about three hours.

I also like pigeon casserole with chestnuts, especially when the weather is really cold. You can't beat this served with Brussels sprouts and mashed potatoes! Pre-heat the oven to around 160°C, 300°F, Gas mark 1. In a large frying pan, melt some butter and add the pigeons to cook them, turning often, for three minutes or so until they are lightly browned all over. Remove the pigeons from the pan and place them in a casserole dish. Add the chestnuts (about four or five per bird). Add garlic and nutmeg to the pan and stir these frequently for a couple of minutes, adding in flour, salt and pepper in the last half minute. I then like to pour in some wine and stock. Take the pan from the heat, and pour the mixture over the pigeons in the casserole. Cover the casserole and put it in the oven for an hour or so until the breasts are really tender when you prick them with a sharp knife. Take the casserole from the oven and serve at once with those sprouts and potatoes. There's nothing better after a cold day in the woods!

20 A PARTING SHOT

This book has been very much for the novice, the lad, the man who wants to know a bit about pigeon shooting, and I have seen it as my duty to teach as much as I can in my own way. I can't think of a better sport for a young person. It is the perfect way to get out and about in the country-side, learn to love it, develop a new skill and find a life-long interest. Providing the young gun is sensible and he has the right sort of tutor, he can't really go wrong. Certainly, that's how I see it, and I'll be forever grateful to the people who taught me. That is why I consented to do this book: to repay the debt I owe them.

I suppose the first man I must mention is Henry, my late father. He was quite a guy, and as I get older people tell me we could pass for broth-ers! He had a varied career and at one stage ran the Post Office at Holkham Hall Estate. Some-where, I actually have a picture of him selling a penny stamp to one of the late Lords of Leices-ter! Henry was a character before he met my mother and calmed down a little bit. Back in the early thirties, he came by £1,100 in a pools win – a fortune in those days. He gave a couple of hundred away and spent the rest on cars, women and general merry-making. In later life, people often asked him if he ever regretted the way he spent his money. His old eyes would just twinkle and he'd give one of his famous grins, and we all knew the answer!

Above all, he was a tremendous fields man and an expert pigeon shooter. Whenever we went out together, he would take a catapult, and rarely came back without an old cock pheasant or two, a hare or some pigeons for the pot. He used to tell me that whenever I was on my own, I should walk as quietly as I could into the wood and I would be amazed by what I saw.

Pigeons fascinated my father, and he often called them the most wily of birds. In fact, we would spend hours together just watching their habits, getting to understand them as best we could. That was all part of the countryside scene for my father.

I was lucky to be living in the countryside, espe-cially having an uncle who was keeper in one of Lord Walpole's Estates over near Itteringham. I was always over there as a lad, making my way past the church, over the river through the woods to his house. It was there that I first met George Lamb – as imposing a man as you're ever likely to meet. I can see him now, coming down that long, dusty lane in his horse and cart to help my father out with the foxes. He was a rare fox man, and in just six weeks cleared thirty out of Mossymere Woods – much to everybody's amazement.

The great thing about horses and carts was that you could get close to animals. Cars are nowhere near as good, but even they are sometimes better than the man on foot. Still, sitting behind a horse, you could get up to almost anything, and George made the best use of that. It was George who started me out pigeon shooting, partly to unload a job from his own shoulders, because ridding farmers of vermin was as high on the list of prior-ities in those days as it is now. He took me around, showed me how to use a gun and added to the knowledge my father had given to me. In short, I was living a full outdoor life then, trekking about the woods and the fields, tickling a few trout from the infant River Bure and thoroughly enjoying myself – setting myself up for life.

I've always had the greatest respect for game-keepers and so should you – especially now as they are becoming guardians of the countryside and not mere preservers of game. Today, my job takes me to various Estates all around the east of

England, and I make it pretty much my first job to get to know the keeper at each one. That's one of the most important bits of advice that I can offer any new shooter: you've got to get off on the right footing with the keeper. If you do, you will be well in for seasons to come. Keepers' lives are much easier now, because they have machinery and motor transport, but in the old days they used to have to be on the rearing field before daylight, and they wouldn't leave until after dark. They had to walk there and back and carry just about everything they wanted to hand. They still knew everything about the countryside and could tell the most amazing tales.

Gamekeepers then and now have always had a soft spot for pigeons. George Lamb used to say that a pigeon was the keeper's best friend. You see, if a keeper goes into a wood at night, and the pigeons get up and flock away, then he knows that nobody has been in the wood before him and there are no poachers about. If, however, the wood is all quiet, then his suspicions are aroused and he gives the area a good check out. It's much the same with the blackbird. If, on his rounds, he hears a blackbird mobbing, then he can be very sure that there is a cat, weasel or stoat about, and he'd better look to it.

Gamekeepers now are really more conservationists than anything else, and they do a lot of good in the countryside. It's a shame there aren't more of them, because when there were, vermin were kept down to an acceptable level and there were songbirds just about everywhere. Today, gamekeepers are very much in decline, and as a result stoats and all the rest are getting the upper hand.

I've concentrated on the country scene in this last chapter, because I think you have to understand pigeon shooting in context if you're going to be successful and really enjoy it. It's very likely that in the course of your career, you will meet some people who disapprove of shooting and aren't afraid to tell you. It's a free country, and you have got to respect their views, but a lot of people who criticize country ways don't really understand them. Shooting has long been part of the country scene, and you've got to remember that a lot of woodlands are protected and cher-

The good pigeon shot will lend anyone a hand. Here the author was contacted by the RSPCA to put a wounded heron out of its misery after breaking its wings on wire.

ished and a lot of birds are reared and let free because of shooting. Shooting pigeons is vital for the farmers, just as if you don't shoot a certain number of deer on the Scottish moors each autumn they will simply perish and die the following winter. The countryman recognizes all these facts and realizes that a sensible man with a gun has an important role to play. This, I think, should be your answer if you ever meet any hostility. Stress that you are not a butcher and that you only shoot what and where is necessary.

In the end, I just hope that this book inspires you to take up shooting and enjoy the pleasure that knowledge of the countryside can bring. Shooting is just a way into appreciating the whole of nature. There is far more to killing a pigeon than simply pulling a trigger.

INDEX